The Architecture of
Historic Richmond

# The Architecture
# of Historic Richmond

**Paul S. Dulaney**

**Second Edition**

The University Press of Virginia
Charlottesville

Copyright © 1968, 1976 by the Rector and Visitors
    of the University of Virginia

First published 1968

The University Press of Virginia

Second edition 1976

*Cover illustration:* Ironwork, Pulliam House


Library of Congress Cataloging in Publication Data

Dulaney, Paul S.
    The architecture of historic Richmond.

    Includes index.
    1. Richmond—Buildings.    2. Architecture—Richmond.
I. Title.
NA735.R5D8    1976        917.55'451'044        68-14089
ISBN 0-8139-0709-8


*Printed in the United States of America*

## Sponsors

Historic Richmond Foundation

The Association for the Preservation of Virginia Antiquities

The William Byrd Branch, APVA

The Valentine Museum

The Planning Commission of the City of Richmond

The Old Dominion Foundation


## Sponsors of the Second Edition

The William Byrd Branch, The Association for the Preservation of Virginia Antiquities

Historic Richmond Foundation

# Acknowledgments

This publication and the survey on which it is based were made possible by the sponsoring organizations listed on page v. In addition special thanks are due to a number of individuals. Previous work of Miss Mary Wingfield Scott through her books and earlier inventory of historic buildings provided invaluable source material. Mrs. Ralph T. Catterall gave helpful advice and criticism, as did Tucker H. Hill of the staff of the Virginia Historic Landmarks Commission. Carlo Pelliccia prepared the maps, made some of the photographs, and gave useful advice throughout.

P. S. D.

Charlottesville, Virginia
March 1968

# Preface to the Second Edition

The untimely death of Paul Dulaney prevents the sponsors from having the second edition prepared under his direction. For this reason changes have been kept to a minimum, being limited to an update on demolished buildings in the inventory listing, a sequel to Chapter III, and the inclusion of an index. The updating of this book also provides the opportunity of acknowledging the contribution of S. Allen Chambers, Jr., and John G. Zehmer, Jr., who carried out the survey upon which this book was based.

Tucker Hill

Richmond
June 1976

# Contents

*Historic Prints and Photographs from the Valentine Museum*

All other photographs were taken by Carlo Pelliccia and the author.

The Architecture of
Historic Richmond

# Chapter I

# The City and Its Architecture

In the spring of 1607 a band of settlers landed on Jamestown Island and established the first English colony in America. Eight days later Captain Christopher Newport led an exploration party up the James River, arriving at the river falls on May 24 and visiting an Indian village where Richmond now stands.

Although one hundred and thirty years went by before the Town of Richmond was staked out just below the James River fall line, this excursion in a sense marks the beginning of the city's history. Settlement of the Virginia Colony was generally not by town building, as in New England, but by plantations, which had direct water access to the mother country. The earlier plantations were mostly along the banks of the James and the other rivers. The river was the artery of transport; its falls marked the end point of this transport, and for many years they marked the frontier of the colony. This was a strategic place for two reasons: as an outpost for trade on the edge of the inland wilderness and for the purposes of defense in an alien environment.

In 1679 Captain William Byrd was granted land near the falls of the James on the condition that he establish a settlement there. The settlement did not materialize in any formal way for nearly sixty years; not until 1737 did his son William Byrd II lay out a town along the north bank of the river, just east of Shockoe Creek. Richmond was incorporated five years later. The town grew slowly at first. When it was chosen as the state capital in 1779, it was a mere village of less than seven hundred people.

Nevertheless it had already achieved a certain prominence in the affairs of the emerging nation. The second Virginia Convention was called together in March 1775 for the purpose of deciding on a course of action to counter the oppressive acts of the British Parliament. The place of the meeting was Richmond, in modest St. John's Church, which is still standing; this location was chosen to be out of the reach of Governor Dunmore in Williamsburg. Here, following the impassioned plea by Patrick Henry, the motion was carried to arm the colony against the royal government.

Within two months the Governor withdrew from Williamsburg; the third convention met there, instructed the Virginia delegates to the Continental Congress to obtain independence, then went about the business of establishing a state government and elected Patrick Henry as first governor. The decision to move the capital from Williamsburg to Richmond was made in 1779. Security from the British troops and the need for a more central location were both factors in the selection of Richmond, which was considered to be "more safe and central than any other town on navigable water."

## Early Architecture

The architectural heritage surviving from the pre-Revolutionary village is slim indeed. There are, at most, two buildings. One of these is St. John's Church, or rather the early part of it, an extremely simple frame structure which is the transept of the church we now see. The Old Stone House on E. Main Street, which today houses the Edgar Allan Poe Museum, is of uncertain date, but it may have been here before the town itself was started. Wood was the common building material and the houses were generally of frame construction covered with clapboards, so the Old Stone House is not a typical house of its time; it may well owe its very survival to its material.

Richmond has two other colonial houses in its outskirts today, but neither was a part of the early city. Ampthill (1732) and Wilton (1753) are Virginia plan-

tation manor houses which have been moved in recent
years from their original sites and rebuilt in Richmond.

The General Assembly convened for the first time in
Richmond in 1780, using temporary quarters on Cary
Street at the foot of Shockoe Hill. Thomas Jefferson had
succeeded Patrick Henry as governor of the Commonwealth when the move to Richmond was made. Jefferson was subsequently called to serve the new nation as
minister to France. While there he was asked by the
state "to consult an able Architect on a plan fit for a
Capitol." As he was later to do in his design for the
University of Virginia, he chose a classical Roman prototype as his model for the state Capitol. The Maison
Carrée, a Roman temple in southern France, was his
model; the Capitol is an enlarged and modified version.
The adaptation and plans were carried out by a French
architect, Charles-Louis Clérisseau. The cornerstone of
the Capitol was laid in 1785 and the Assembly held its
first session there three years later.

The Capitol was Richmond's first building of monumental scale. It was built of brick covered with stucco to
simulate stone. Jefferson's building is the central portion
of the present structure; the wings were added at the
start of this century.

There are a very few buildings standing in Richmond
today that are, more or less, contemporary with the
Capitol. These are widely scattered, and also varied in
use and appearance; they do not lend themselves to any
kind of neat stylistic classification. Two of them, of
exceptional value in the city's heritage, might be described as late Georgian: the John Marshall house
(1788-90), an example of a gentleman's dwelling and
the oldest brick house in the city, and Masons' Hall
(1787) on Franklin Street in Shockoe Valley, a frame
building with hipped roof and cupola. The other four
are frame and clapboard dwellings and they show two
versions of the vernacular, that is, the commonplace
everyday building of the time. The restored Craig house
(c. 1784) and the Daniel Call house (before 1796), altered and relocated, share an extremely simple farm-
house quality. An even more modest kind of dwelling

survives in two gambrel-roofed cottages at 612 and
1013 N. Third Street (c. 1800 and 1790).

Richmond had been chartered as a city in 1782. As
state capital it had new stimulus for growth. The population in 1790 was only 3,761; in 1800, it had grown to
5,730. During the first two decades of the new century
there was a marked increase in commercial and industrial activity. Tobacco and grain production had from
the earliest days been an important function of the Virginia Colony. Now around the turn of the century
manufactures began increasing in importance. Corn and
wheat flour, cotton textiles, soap, candles, and carriages
were produced by Richmond factories. Tobacco manufacturing, which was to become so important to the city's
economy later in the century, was also substantial. By
1820 the population of Richmond had grown to 12,067.
Other factors contributing to the development of trade
during this period were the organization and growth of
banking and transportation improvements in the form of
turnpikes, as well as the beginning of a canal system.

## Latrobe and Mills

Around the turn of the century several Richmond buildings were designed by Benjamin H. Latrobe, an English-
born architect who has been called the father of the
architectural profession in America. His American career
started in Virginia, his commissions coming first in Norfolk, then in Richmond. Unfortunately, none of his
Richmond buildings remain. His chief work here was
the state penitentiary (1797-1800), built on the site
where that institution still operates. At the same time he
designed a mansion for Colonel John Harvie. Shortly
afterward it was sold to Robert Gamble; the site is now
known as Gamble's Hill. Another Latrobe mansion, an
extremely handsome one, was built (1808-9) on Council Chamber Hill, east of Capitol Square and overlooking Shockoe Valley. Latrobe also designed a magnificent
theater for Richmond (1798), but it was never built.
The design of this building, and his others as well, is

known through the architect's precise water-color draw-
ings preserved in the Library of Congress.

The buildings of the 1800-1820 decades which remain
to be seen and enjoyed today were almost all designed as

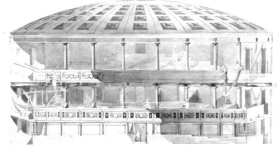

*Latrobe Theater*

residences; an important exception is Monumental
Church (1814) on Broad Street, designed by Robert
Mills. Mills, a pupil of Latrobe, became an architect
of national prominence, designing many public buildings
in Philadelphia, Washington, Baltimore, and elsewhere.
His presence in Richmond in connection with the design
of this church resulted in further commissions. He was
retained to design the city hall. This was built in 1816,
after some design revision by Maximilian Godefroy,
facing Capitol Square on the north side; this fine classical
building was razed after 1870 and replaced by the mas-

*City Hall of 1816*

sive stone Victorian City Hall which now stands on the site of the earlier building. Mills was also the designer of the Wickham house (1812), now part of the Valentine Museum, and the Brockenbrough house (1816-18), which became the White House of the Confederacy and is now the Confederate Museum. A number of other mansions of the same decade, now gone, have also been attributed to him. In any case, the influence of this noted architect was considerable in Richmond.

## The Federal Style

After the fire of 1787 brick began to replace wood frame as the prevalent wall construction in Richmond dwellings, at least for the homes of the professional classes. Characteristic of the 1800-1820 period are the brick lintels over the windows, plastered over to simulate stone, with a "keystone" in the center. The Flemish bond pattern of brickwork (alternate bricks being turned endwise for better bonding) was commonly used in this era, a continuation of earlier colonial practice. These features can be seen at the Hancock-Caskie house (1808-9) on Fifth Street at Main and the Crozet house (1814-15) on Main Street at First. Both are fine houses which have found contemporary uses in transition areas of downtown Richmond.

For a time after 1810 it was not uncommon for the entire brick exterior to be covered with stucco, giving the appearance of stone from a distance. Examples of this practice are the White House of the Confederacy, the Wickham house, and Carrington Row (1818) on Church Hill. Other façade embellishments characteristic of the period were recessed arches framing windows (Wickham house), recessed panels between windows, triple windows (Wickham house, Governor's Mansion, and White House of the Confederacy), and pilasters (Carrington Row). All of these features were used on the front of the Union Hotel (1817), pulled down early in the present century. That interesting building was the creation of Otis Manson, the first professional architect to live in Richmond.

The finer Richmond houses of this period had verandas on the garden side, monumental porticos with classical columns; these are features of the two surviving Mills mansions. The garden of the White House of the

*Union Hotel, at 19th and Main Streets*

Confederacy has been restored, and that of the Wickham house is certainly one of the most pleasant spaces in the city today. The Archer-Anderson house (1816), next to the Jefferson Hotel on Franklin Street, has a two-story portico in the rear, the only feature of the original design to escape the debasement of alterations made in the late nineteenth century.

Economic depression struck in 1819. Home construction was immediately retarded and remained at a consistently low level for the next two decades. It revived with a sudden boom in the year 1840, and thereafter building activity was relatively brisk until it was virtually stopped at the outbreak of the Civil War.

## Transportation and Industry

Actually transportation developments in the thirties had set the stage for the lively industrial progress of the ensuing two decades. The canal, which was constructed to by-pass the river falls, had been opened in 1789, but it then remained as only a local operation for many years. In 1835 the company was reorganized as the

James River and Kanawha Company, and by 1851 the canal was completed to Buchanan, nearly 200 miles west. Improvements were also made to the city's dock facilities, and regular steamboat service operated between Richmond, Norfolk, and Baltimore.

Richmond's first steam railroad was chartered in 1834 as the Richmond, Fredericksburg and Potomac. In eight years the line had been extended to Aquia Creek, on the Potomac, where connection was made by boat to Washington. Other lines were established radiating out from Richmond; by the start of the Civil War, railroads had been built west across the Blue Ridge to Clifton Forge, southwest to Danville, and south to Petersburg, with connections to Norfolk and Tennessee. In 1859 the canal traffic accounted for more freight than all four of the city's railroads together, but the water carrier could not long compete with the steam trains, and twenty years later the canal boats had passed into history.

Flour milling, tobacco manufacturing, and iron and foundry works were the foremost industries. Water power for the grist mills had early made Richmond an important center for the manufacture of flour, and this continued to be an important industry until late in the nineteenth century. The largest mills were those of Gallego at the east end of the canal basin and Haxall (later Haxall and Crenshaw) to the south along the river. Old prints of the city show their towering buildings as prominent features of the skyline. One of the Haxall structures is still standing at Twelfth and Byrd Streets; close by are the massive granite foundations of another.

Richmond became one of the world's leading centers of tobacco products; in 1859 the city had forty-three tobacco factories employing 2,388 workers. Two quite handsome factories built for tobacco processing remain today on E. Franklin Street: the Grant factory at Nineteenth Street, designed by the architect Samuel Freeman, and the Yarbrough (now Pohlig) factory at Twenty-fifth Street, by John Freeman, his brother.

Stimulated by improved means of transport for raw materials, and also by the direct demand for products created by the new railroads, iron production and fabri-

*Gallego Flour Mills*

cation were greatly expanded. The Tredegar Iron Works, established in 1838, was the largest producer. The remains of its buildings are at the foot of Gamble's Hill.

Relatively few houses were built during the 1820's and the early 1830's. These residences were generally quite simple and, in the detailing of the trim, cornices, and entrance porches, retained a lightness and grace that was characteristic of the previous two decades. Examples of brick residences of the period may be seen in the Addolph Dill house (1832) at oo Clay Street and on Church Hill at 405 N. Twenty-seventh Street (1835) and the Andrew Ellett house (1829). Recently restored are two frame cottages of the early thirties at the corner of Twenty-fifth and E. Grace Streets, opposite St. John's Churchyard. There is also a commercial building from this time which retains its original form, the Wortham and Magruder warehouse (1830) on the northeast corner of Fifteenth and E. Cary Streets.

Isaiah Rogers was the architect of a fine hotel erected in the early boom years of the forties. The Exchange Hotel (1841, demolished 1900) stood at Franklin and

*Exchange Hotel*

Fourteenth Streets; its handsome façade showed a strikingly original adaptation from classical sources. Rogers, one of America's most talented building designers, had already become noted as a hotel architect in Boston and New York; he subsequently designed most of the largest and most important hotels built in the South and West up until the Civil War.

## Greek Revival Architecture

Of all of the nineteenth-century architectural styles, the one called Greek Revival has left the strongest imprint on the Richmond cityscape. As a façade treatment for dwellings now standing it is first discernible in structures of about 1836; during the 1840-50 decade it was the all-pervading fashion. Although a romantic counterpoint came on the scene in the fifties, the Greek influence continued dominant until the Civil War. This influence was in fact country-wide in scope; for the mid-decades of the century the Greek Revival was virtually a national style, tempered with regional variations.

One form of the Greek Revival residence, used extensively for mansions elsewhere, was not common in Richmond. This was the temple form, employing a monumental portico with columns two stories high. There were two such houses in Richmond, built in 1845 opposite each other on W. Franklin Street. One of these, the Anderson house, was torn down to make way for the Jefferson Hotel. The other one, the Mayo house, survives, but with the wings raised to two stories and the windows altered, its original appearance is considerably changed.

In general, the Greek Revival house has a heavier and more masculine appearance than its predecessors of the Federal period, with wider trim and simpler moldings. In the Richmond vernacular the chief feature is a small porch framing the entranceway, with wood columns and pediment using one of the Greek orders and ornament with Greek motifs; the porch commonly has a granite base and steps. The window lintels are usually plain and rectilinear, sometimes of granite, or they may be faced with a wood facia shaped to suggest a pediment. Cast-iron fences with these houses may also echo Greek ornamental motifs. Several early examples of dwellings in this style may be seen near the intersection of Foushee and Main Streets, the Ellen Glasgow house (1841) on the southwest corner being the best preserved of these. (The Quarles house, which was built in 1839 and stood opposite at the southeast corner, was demolished in February 1968.) The interesting double house (1836) across the street at 4-6 E. Main Street has been brutally marred by a store addition in front. Outstanding houses in the Greek Revival style, in immaculate condition, include the Bransford-Cecil Memorial house (1840), rebuilt as part of the Valentine Museum on E. Clay Street, and the Scott-Clarke (1841) and Barret (1844) houses, which stand side by side on Fifth Street south of Main and are used as offices. On Church Hill the style is typified by restored houses at 2300 E. Grace Street and 2300 E. Broad Street, both built at mid-century, while the nearby Turpin and Yarbrough houses (1861) at 2209 and 2215 E. Broad are examples of the late use of the style.

There are many other fine Greek Revival dwellings in Richmond, on Church Hill and elsewhere. Certainly one of the most valuable things in the city's architectural heritage is the town house group known as Linden Row (1847-53) in the 100 block of E. Franklin Street. This row originally extended the full length of the block; eight of the original ten dwellings survive today in an area no longer residential. They compose a street façade of extraordinary quality.

Before the Greek Revival fashion had run its course an architectural reaction set in against its staid dignity. Stylistic labels have been given to a variety of other revivals which came into vogue during the fifties: Gothic Revival, Italianate, and others. They had in common a departure from classical models and a tendency toward ornateness and exuberant expression, qualities which eventually ran riot in the latter half of the Victorian era. Richmond does not have a large heritage of such buildings from the 1850's, but several are striking in appearance, and the uniqueness of each in the city makes them valuable landmarks. Among these are: Morson Row (1853), a group of three town houses with curved fronts, closing the vista at the east end of Capitol Street; the William H. Grant house (1857), which served as the Sheltering Arms Hospital from 1892 until 1965; and the Bolling Haxall house (1858) at 211 E. Franklin, home of the Woman's Club since 1900.

Also notable are the two Putney houses (1861 and 1859) at 1010 and 1012 E. Marshall Street. These are especially distinguished by the ornamental ironwork, the one on the corner having a two-story iron veranda of exceptional quality. A distinctive building which marks an early departure from the Greek Revival influence is the Egyptian Building (1845) at the corner of E. Marshall and College Streets, the first building constructed for the medical school which is now the Medical College of Virginia.

## Ornamental Iron

The ironwork of Richmond is a superb feature of its nineteenth-century architecture from 1819, when Paul-Alexis Sabbaton designed the fence around Capitol Square, until iron verandas went out of fashion around 1885. The portion of this artistry that survives continues to contribute a special quality to the city today. Richmond's ornamental metal is very largely cast iron rather than wrought iron. To a considerable extent it was produced by local foundries.

Fences make up the earlier examples of ironwork, together with gates and porch railings. These were a frequent adornment around the small front yards of Greek Revival houses: the Barret and Norman Stewart houses and Linden Row are three examples from many which still exist. Thomas Stewart, the Philadelphia architect who designed the Egyptian Building and St. Paul's Church, created custom designs for the fences of each of these buildings. Shockoe Cemetery, the Hebrew Cemetery close by, and the later Hollywood Cemetery all contain a wealth of fine iron fences and gates. Probably the most elaborate creation in ornamental iron is the Gothic monument which marks President Monroe's tomb in Hollywood; it was designed by architect Albert Lybrock in the 1850's.

Cast-iron trim for windows, doors, and cornices came into extensive use in the late fifties, and for commercial buildings whole fronts were fabricated by the foundries. A fine decorative example of the iron trim on a residence is the Samuel Putney house (1859) at 1010 E. Marshall Street. The most striking of the architectural iron features were the verandas, which also came into fashion during the fifties, supplanting the small porches of the Greek Revival period. The vogue for these was widespread and they were extensively used up into the 1880's, for modest homes as well as mansions. The great variety of intricate patterns can still be seen today in the older neighborhoods of Richmond, from Church Hill to the Fan District.

## Notable Churches

The churches built in Richmond between 1830 and the Civil War present a varied array of architectural styles and they are without exception valuable and impressive landmarks. Only two churches survive from earlier days: historic St. John's and Robert Mills's Monumental Church.

St. Peters, E. Grace at Eighth Street, designed in the Classic Revival manner, was built in 1834 and served as the cathedral for the Richmond Diocese of the Roman Catholic Church until after the turn of the century. First Baptist Church (1841) on Broad at Twelfth Street is a Greek temple in form, and its design probably influenced the later African Baptist Church on College Street at Broad. The First Baptist Church is the only Richmond work of Thomas U. Walter, who designed the dome and wings of the U.S. Capitol.

St. Paul's Episcopal Church (1845) on Grace Street at Capitol Square is the most ornate of the mid-century churches. It too is classical, but with Georgian antecedents: its prototype is St. Luke's in Philadelphia. This was the church of Jefferson Davis and Robert E. Lee during the Civil War. Second Presbyterian on Fifth Street north of Main was built two years later in a vastly different style; this was Richmond's first building in the new Gothic Revival manner. The architect was Minard Lafever of New York. Broad Street Methodist (1858-59) and Trinity Methodist (1861), on E. Broad at Tenth and Twentieth Streets respectively, similar churches by the Richmond architect, Albert L. West, are again departures from classical design models and show Italianate characteristics. These two churches, as well as St. Paul's, were once capped by spires, which have been removed. A fine classical church of the period is Leigh Street Baptist (1853) on Twenty-fifth Street, designed by Samuel Sloan of Philadelphia.

## The Civil War and After

Richmond's tragic role in the War between the States is a familiar story. In May 1861, the month following the outbreak of war, the city was chosen to be the capital of the Confederate States of America. Because of this and also because of the industrial importance of the city, especially in armaments, Richmond was a prime military objective of the Union forces throughout the war. In 1862 attempts to take the city both by river gunboats and by land were repulsed. Some of the battles with McClellan's forces were joined so close to the city that the fighting could be seen from the rooftops. In the final year of the war Richmond was under a virtual

*Ruins of Richmond, April 1865*

state of siege and her citizens suffered great privation. During the conflict many of the tobacco warehouses were used as hospitals, some as prisons. The Northern troops did not succeed in occupying the city until the whole Confederate military structure had collapsed from fatigue and attrition.

President Davis and his government left Richmond three days before the final surrender at Appomattox; on the morning of Sunday, April 2, 1865, while attending services at St. Paul's, he received a message from General Lee advising him to leave the city without delay. The evacuation fire which started on the night of that April Sunday was one of the great dramas in the history of Richmond. The fires were started when several warehouses were ignited in order to deprive the enemy of the goods stored in them. There was rioting and looting, and the conflagrations spread uncontrolled. The chief part of the business district was wiped out; a wide area from Capitol Square south to the river was in ruins.

Virginia suffered the indignities of Reconstruction for five years. In 1870 the Commonwealth was again a state in the Union, with its own elected government. The same year Richmond was the scene of two disasters and, in addition, suffered its greatest flood in a hundred years. During a hearing of the Court of Appeals, a floor in the Capitol collapsed, killing 62 people and injuring 250. At Christmas, the city's newest hotel, the Spotswood at Eighth and Main Streets, was destroyed by

*Spotswood Hotel*

fire. The inn had been built shortly before the war; it had narrowly escaped the evacuation fire which burnt out the blocks adjacent to the north and east.

In the years from 1870 to 1900, Richmond revived as a commercial and manufacturing center. Soon after the war rail connection to Washington and thus to the industrial northeast was completed, and the Chesapeake and Ohio was extended west through the West Virginia coal fields. A Chamber of Commerce yearbook in 1893 could claim that Richmond was the second manufacturing city of the South (next to Louisville). The growing popularity of cigarettes was a stimulus to the tobacco industry, which continued to be the leading manufacturing enterprise. In 1885 the making of tobacco products employed over 7,000 workers in the city. Other important industries included foundry and machine shops, fertilizer manufacturing, printing and publishing, and the production of paper boxes, wagons and carriages, and leather goods. By the end of the century the population had more than doubled from the prewar figure; the census showed a total of 85,050 inhabitants in 1900.

## Cast-iron Commercial Buildings

The rebuilding of downtown Richmond after the evacuation fire was done rapidly. Main Street between Eighth and Fifteenth Streets thus acquired a building façade in the fashion of a single decade. The result was homogeneous in scale, materials, and height, yet quite varied in detail. The dominant material was cast iron; it was

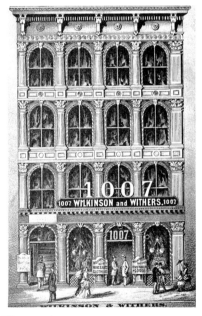

*Iron-front building, 1007 E. Main*

fabricated and molded into ornamental shapes, usually imitating classical decorative elements. Cast-iron fronts were widely used on commercial buildings in American cities during the Civil War decade; the fire simply set the stage for an unusual concentration of these buildings in Richmond while the style was in vogue. Because commercial structures tend to have a high rate of obsolescence, the cast-iron architecture across the land has largely disappeared. Richmond, a hundred years later, still has a residue of this past, enough to give some individuality at least to a few blocks of E. Main Street, although a number of the survivals have been defaced by insensitive remodeling. The commercial blocks at 1007-13 and 1207-11 are choice examples of the period.

## The Late Nineteenth Century

Richmond had much residential building in the late Victorian era, the last three decades of the nineteenth century. The lower part of the Fan District was developed at this time, and it illustrates well the characteristic domestic architecture of the period. The blocks of W. Franklin Street just west of Monroe Park are typical; while the individual buildings are hardly handsome, the over-all effect is good. These city blocks are part of Richmond's time dimension and history, and the cityscape would be poorer without them. The Ginter mansion (1890) of brick and brownstone is a choice example of a wealthy citizen's residence in that era of individualism.

In the Sydney neighborhood south of Monroe Park, and elsewhere, may be seen the houses of the working people of this time. The dwellings may be of brick or wood frame; in either case there is usually some ornamental woodwork, typically bracketed cornices, and front porches decorated with patterns cut by the scroll saw.

The prevailing Victorian taste left its mark on many houses built in an earlier period. Frequently this modernizing obliterated superior architecture. The oldest house now standing on W. Franklin Street is the Archer-Anderson house, just east of the Jefferson Hotel. It was built in 1816, but the addition of the third story and complete remodeling of the façade in 1881 have made it both Victorian and ugly; the sole exterior remnant of the original design is the two-story elliptical porch in back. Some changes, however, were not so damaging. The White-Taylor house (1839) on Church Hill at 2717 E. Grace also had alterations in 1881, including an added story on top. But the changes did not erase all of the original character of the house, and they contributed a side veranda of exquisite ornamental iron.

Monument Avenue had its beginning in the 1890's. Here Richmond has, as part of its city plan, a street of exceptional visual quality. The name was given to this extension of Franklin Street in 1890, when the memorial to Robert E. Lee was placed at the Allen Street intersection. This was then at the edge of the city; a photograph of the unveiling shows a panorama of bare fields. The avenue, with its commodious width and central planting space, was laid out at that time. Four other

*Unveiling of the Lee Monument*

monuments honoring Confederate heroes were subsequently placed in the center at intervals along its
course, between 1907 and 1929.

Six buildings in Richmond, public and commercial,
illustrate the varied architectural tastes toward the end
of the century. The massive granite City Hall was begun
in 1887 and completed seven years later. The office
building at the northeast corner of Governor and Main
Streets was built in 1893 as the Planters National Bank.
This is Richmond's only large building remaining as an
example of the Romanesque Revival style, which was
introduced by the New England architect H. H. Richardson and which had wide popularity in the decades
after the Civil War. The Commonwealth Club (1890)
on W. Franklin Street echoes both Romanesque and
Italian Renaissance mannerisms; the use of decorative
terra-cotta trim was in vogue for a few years before and
after 1890. Two blocks east on Franklin Street is the
Jefferson Hotel, the city's foremost landmark of this era.
It was opened in 1895, partially burned after 1900, and
rebuilt. The architects, Carrère and Hastings, endowed
it with Spanish and Italian Renaissance forms and decoration and grandiose interior public spaces.

The Henrico County Court House (1896) is more
modestly lavish, though it shows the masonry furbelows,
both in brick and stone, that characterize the building
practice of the nineties. Finally, the new century was
ushered in by the completion of Main Street Station
(1900) in Shockoe Valley, a French Provincial palace
built by the Chesapeake and Ohio Railway to provide
for itself a fitting monumental entrance to the capital
city. The great iron train shed connected to it is entirely
utilitarian; in it we may find a truer symbol of the
structural achievements of the nineteenth century.

## The Twentieth Century

Richmond's story in the twentieth century is highlighted
by accelerated growth and change. It shares this experience
with most other American cities; in the first half of the
century the population of the United States doubled.

By the census of 1950, Richmond had 219,958 inhabitants; the metropolitan area had over 400,000.

The changes wrought on central Richmond in these years have come largely from two forces: commercial growth and the automobile. An expanded retail and office district naturally came about to support the greater population. In the early decades of this century this expansion came very largely downtown; the suburban shopping centers are a more recent phenomenon. At the beginning of the century Grace and Franklin Streets were part of the city's best residential district, which extended west from Capitol Square, while a still proud neighborhood stood along the crosstown streets out to Gamble's Hill. At the time of the First World War, Grace Street began to convert to a shopping street and the transition on Franklin Street set in sometime later. The old residences fell away like dominoes from this commercial thrust. The downtown part of Grace Street retains no trace of its former character. A similar kind of commercial transition is now happening in a neighborhood of humbler nineteenth-century homes centered on Clay and Leigh Streets from Eighth Street west.

The impact of the automobile on the twentieth-century city is so evident that it needs no considerable description. It has by no means run its course. The vast amount of land preempted for expressways, interchanges, and vehicle storage in the form of parking lots and structures works drastic changes on the face of the city.

The eclectic approach to building design that was established in the nineties continued through the first three decades of the twentieth century. This reflected the influence of the Paris Ecole des Beaux-Arts, first transmitted through some of our native architects who went there for their training, then made universal by the adoption of its educational system by American schools of architecture. It is an oversimplification to say that architectural design was divorced from the engineering science of structure, but this was really at the root of the matter. In any case all American architects who had formal training up, at least, until the mid-1930's were indoctrinated with a philosophy of design which held that the historic styles, evolved in past ages for past conditions of society, use, materials, and technology, were appropriate expressions for modern buildings.

Monumental buildings in Richmond of the early twentieth century, following Main Street Station, include: Sacred Heart Cathedral (1904) at Monroe Park; Broad Street Station (1917-19), designed by John Russell Pope in a Roman manner which had proven adaptable to rail terminals; and the Mosque (1928), also facing Monroe Park. The bizarre Near Eastern decor that bedecks the Mosque may be attributed to the fact that the building was designed as a Shrine temple.

Today an array of technological advances and inventions shapes the design of our buildings and the form of our cities. The nineteenth-century inventions of the elevator and steel skeleton construction injected a new scale into urban architecture and, together with the pressure of land values, created the present-day skylines of New York and Chicago. A major significance of the skeleton frame, whether of steel or ferro-concrete, was that the walls of the building no longer supported the structure; the material of the walls, whether of stone, metal panels, or glass, became a curtain or facing which was attached to the supporting structural framework. Although there were early and exciting departures in the architectural treatment of tall office buildings, notably in Chicago, the Beaux-Arts design philosophy was so embedded in the thinking of architects that for many decades most skeleton-frame buildings were decorated with classical, or sometimes Gothic, ornament. In Richmond the First and Merchants Bank building (1912) on E. Main Street at Ninth typifies office building design of the early twentieth century.

Since World War II, and especially in the sixties, there has been a surge of rebuilding in the downtown area. The bulk of this construction has been privately financed office buildings, but the state is currently a substantial entrepreneur, with tall structures going up at the Medical College, in the expansion of government offices east of Capitol Square, and in the continuing development

of the Richmond Professional Institute in the neighborhood of Monroe Park.

No attempt is made in the present volume to appraise
the individual contemporary buildings of central Richmond. Many of them are commonplace; a few are handsome. All of them share a plain, usually somewhat stark
character. What variety they have comes in the play of
fenestration, the proportioning of window area with curtain wall, the choice of materials and color for windows,
spandrels, and facing. The regional distinctions that
once prevailed in architecture are now largely gone;
there is no place for local character in the building technology of today. Thus Richmond as time goes on looks
more and more like other cities, like any other city. It
is true that an occasional architectural tour de force can
bring real identity to a city. The great steel arch on the
waterfront does this for St. Louis. But such creations are
rare. Richmond's real identity, its character as a unique
place on the face of the earth, still resides in Capitol
Square, in Shockoe Slip, and on Church Hill. It seems
that a great portion of the value of this architectural
heritage, this residue of the past, is that it gives to the city
vivid quality, identity, and meaning. The aim of this
book is to reveal something of this heritage.

# Chapter II

# Historic Areas

*View of Richmond from Church Hill*

# Shockoe Valley

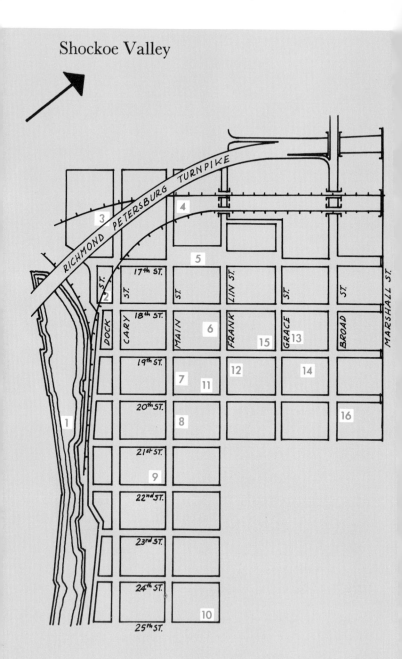

# Shockoe Valley

The shape of the land underlying Richmond is one of hills and creek valleys. Shockoe Creek flows through a ravine east of the city's present-day central area; from the creek bottom the land rises steeply to the Capitol site on the west and to Church Hill on the east.

The town was originally laid out in 1737 on the ground east of Shockoe Creek. When it was incorporated in 1742, it extended east to Twenty-fifth Street and from the James River shore north to Broad Street. Thus the first town boundaries reached out to embrace the eminence of Church Hill, but the early buildings were mostly con-

*View of Shockoe Valley from Church Hill, 1853*

centrated along the river and the lower slopes.

As we look on this oldest section of the city today, what we see is largely a product of the nineteenth century. There are only three buildings left from before 1800; and though there are some new tobacco factories and a scattering of recent store fronts, most of the buildings date from before 1900.

No trace of the early village character is apparent today, except perhaps in the rural atmosphere of the restored Craig house. There are some forlorn remnants that
attest to the neighborhood quality of a later past, mostly
on Nineteenth Street near Grace. Otherwise commerce
and industry have taken over. From the earliest days, of
course, commerce was part of the life of the town. The
site first allotted for markets and fairs has even continued
as a market place for farm produce until the present.

By the early nineteenth century, Main Street was
characterized by rows of brick buildings, with stores at
street level and living quarters above. Two blocks to the
south, the waterfront was the busy scene of shipping
activity. Tobacco manufacturing, which began in this
area, expanded enormously during the middle years of
the century; it continues today to be centered here. The
middle years also saw the coming of the steam railroad.
Shockoe Valley and the low banks of the James provided
suitable terrain for it, and the character of future development of valley and river banks was stamped when
the tracks were laid down.

THE RICHMOND DOCK                                    1

The earliest port development was at Rocketts, down
river from the basin which was developed in the early
nineteenth century as the Richmond Dock. The dock,

which became the city's chief shipping terminal, was created from a backwater of the James, with connection to the river by means of a lock at the foot of Twenty-sixth Street. The existing lock there was built in 1854, replacing an earlier one. Sometime after 1840 a connection was made from the west end of the dock to the canal basin, which was between Eighth and Twelfth Streets south of Cary Street, and the dock then served as a transshipping point between river vessels and canal boats.

John Enders was one of the chief entrepreneurs of the development of the Richmond Dock over almost half a century. At mid-century the dock was lined with warehouses along the south side of Cary Street. One of the Enders warehouses, at the foot of Twentieth Street, was rented by Luther Libby at the outbreak of the Civil War. When it was taken over as a prison, his sign remained on the building, and it became famous as Libby Prison.

It was later dismantled and rebuilt in Chicago, where it had a brief existence as a World's Fair attraction in 1893.

The ante-bellum frame of buildings along the dock has long been gone; an elevated railroad track replaces it, together with junk yards and parking lots, while Richmond's tobacco row makes the building façade on the north side of Cary Street.

PHILIP MORRIS WAREHOUSES      2

*18th Street at Cary*
*early 20th century*

These two brick warehouses are exceptionally fine: here is American industrial architecture at its best.

## CHARLES WHITLOCK STORE    3
*1523 E. Cary Street*
*1812 (demolished 1974)*

Originally a store with dwelling above, this is the only example of this once common building type of the early 1800's now left in Shockoe Valley. It has been mutilated by removal of the attic story with its steep gable and dormers. Window lintels of this shape are typical of the period; in this building they are of stone rather than the plaster imitation that was more commonly used.

## MAIN STREET STATION    4
*E. Main Street between 15th and 17th*
*1900*
*architects: Wilson, Harris and Richards (Philadelphia)*

Built in the heyday of the railroads as passenger carriers, this monumental structure symbolizes the importance of the rail terminal as an entrance gateway to the city. It

is also significant as a fine example of the French influence on architectural design in America through the Beaux-Arts tradition. The working part of the station, the utilitarian iron train shed, is an important survival from the age of steam.

Today the expressway stalks the valley on giant stilts and almost subdues the station, but not quite. From below there is a quite accidental visual excitement that comes from this strange juxtaposition.

*Market House in 1865*

## MARKET SQUARE 5

*17th Street between E. Main and E. Franklin Streets*

This has been a market place since the town was first settled. In those early days there was a "common," a public open space, between the market place and Shockoe Creek and a footbridge over the creek.

Throughout most of Richmond's history some kind of a market structure occupied the central space. In the early days this was a wooden shed. In 1794 a brick building with a colonnade was built, to be replaced by a larger market in 1854. Both of these market houses had a hall on the second floor, used for public meetings. The last market was built in 1913 and was recently replaced by the present metal shed.

As urban space, the market square has suffered from

recent demolition, but the frame of nineteenth-century commercial buildings has good scale and harmony, and the street vistas seen from it are exciting. Scott's Drug Store on the west side at Franklin Street has operated in this building for over a century.

MASONS' HALL                                    6
*1805 E. Franklin Street*
*1787*

A valuable landmark both for its architecture and historical associations, this is one of a very few buildings in Richmond surviving from the eighteenth century. It is also the oldest Masonic lodge in continuous use in the United States. George Washington and John Marshall were among its members; Edmund Randolph was its first Grand Master and Lafayette was an honorary member.

OLD STONE HOUSE          7

*1916 E. Main Street*
*before 1783*

This is the oldest dwelling now standing in Richmond. Its exact date is unknown but in all probability it was built before the Revolutionary War and may possibly have existed before the town was founded. Stone was such an unusual building material in Richmond that this was known as "The Stone House" even in the eighteenth century.

This valuable building was saved from demolition in 1911 and presented to the Association for the Preservation of Virginia Antiquities. It is now maintained by the Edgar Allan Poe Foundation as a museum of books and mementoes relating to the poet, who lived and worked in Richmond. Although there is no known historical association between Poe and this house, he was editor of the *Southern Literary Messenger* which had offices a few blocks west on Main Street.

FIRE  STATION                                                          8
*2000 block of E. Main Street*
*1899*

An unusual bit of civic design, contemporary with
Main Street Station, this building is now used as a warehouse.

HENRICO COUNTY COURT HOUSE                        9
*E. Main Street at 22nd Street*
*1896*

The  seat  of  county  government  has  been  in  this  immediate vicinity since before Richmond became a city. This is the third court house, replacing one built in 1825. The building is a period piece with typical characteristics of 1890 masonry practice: corbeled brickwork, stone trim, variety of window treatment.

## THREE TOBACCO FACTORIES

Here are three mid-century industrial structures built for tobacco processing. There were five such factories built in this area during the year 1853 alone. These three are still in use either as factories or as warehouses. The Grant factory was used during the Civil War first as a barracks, then as a hospital.

YARBROUGH-POHLIG FACTORY 10
*2419 E. Franklin Street*
*1853*
*architect: John Freeman*

JOHN ENDERS FACTORY                    11
*20-26 N. 20th Street*
*1849*

WM. H. GRANT FACTORY                   12
*1900 E. Franklin Street*
*1853*
*architect: Samuel Freeman*

CRAIG HOUSE                                            13
*1812 E. Grace Street*
*c. 1784-87*

This is considered to be the second-oldest dwelling house in Richmond and is the oldest built of wood. Adam Craig, who built it, was a prominent public official. His daughter, Jane Craig Stanard, born here, was immortalized as the "Helen" of Edgar Allan Poe.

When destruction of this house was imminent in 1935, the William Byrd Branch of the Association for the Preservation of Virginia Antiquities was created and succeeded in saving it. They have subsequently restored it.

N. 19TH STREET
*100 and 200 blocks*

The Craig house stands at the south end of a block which is now largely made up of dwellings of the middle and late nineteenth century. However, the Talbot house (1850), 201 N. Nineteenth Street, in the Greek Revival style with a handsome Ionic portico on a granite base, was demolished in the spring of 1967. Its neighbor to the north, at 205 N. Nineteenth Street, was built ten years later and shows the change in taste that came during the fifties from staid dignity to exuberance: the ornate ironwork has a Moorish quality to it.

The next block south has sadly changed. The industrial intrusions are ugly and brutal; the old houses are decayed and have a ghostly look. The double house on the corner, 1813-15 E. Grace Street, and the house at 113 N. Nineteenth Street were built in the second decade of the 1800's. Characteristic of their time, these houses have steep gable roofs, plaster keystone lintels over the windows, and brickwork in Flemish bond pattern.

PACE-KING HOUSE          14
*205 N. 19th Street*
*1860*

CRUMP DOUBLE HOUSE          15
*1813-15 E. Grace Street*
*1818*

TRINITY METHODIST CHURCH                    16
*E. Broad and 20th Streets*
*1861*
*architect: Albert L. West*

This church, in the Italianate style, is similar to the same
architect's Broad Street Methodist Church, but it is less
elaborate. West was a local architect who also remodeled, in Gothic style, Centenary Church on Grace
Street. Trinity Church had a spire which was removed
after hurricane damage in 1954.

*Southern Fertilizing Company (formerly Libby Prison)*

# Church Hill

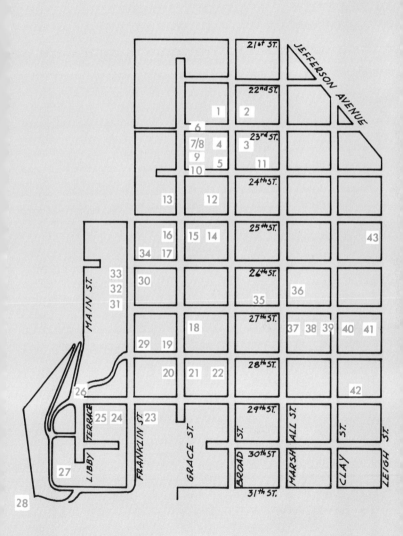

## Church Hill

The village of Richmond grew in time from its river front and valley site onto the two heights to the east and west. Church Hill was earlier called Indian Town and then Richmond Hill; the modern name comes from the simple frame church (now St. John's) which was built there above the village in 1741. Today Church Hill as a neighborhood has rather uncertain boundaries but may be considered for convenience as extending from Twentieth Street to Twenty-ninth Street and Libby Terrace and from Franklin north to Jefferson Avenue.

Although Church Hill is popularly, and mistakenly, thought of as the oldest part of Richmond, actually it was not intensively settled until the first decades of the nineteenth century. Before that the community consisted of the church itself and the rural holdings of the Richard Adams family and a few others. Certainly the choice of Shockoe Hill, west of the valley, as the site for the Capitol had much to do with the direction of city growth to the west, consequently retarding development on Church Hill.

If Church Hill seems to be the oldest part of Richmond today, it is because more of the past has been retained there. It has been outside of the main thrust of the city's commercial growth and has continued to be essentially a neighborhood of residences. Thus destruction and rebuilding have been less frequent than in other sections of central Richmond. But by the 1950's the area had deteriorated badly. A revival is now under way, chiefly due to the activities of the Historic Richmond Foundation. Church Hill is, potentially, the Richmond equivalent of Georgetown in Washington and Beacon Hill in Boston.

TURPIN AND YARBROUGH HOUSES                    1
*2209 and 2215 E. Broad Street*
*1861*

These almost identical houses were built in the same
year by men who were partners in the tobacco business.
They are characteristic of the late Greek Revival style
in the use of bracket cornices, Ionic porticoes, granite
porches and steps, long living room windows, and flat
roofs. The Turpin house is shown.

2204-6, 2208-10 AND 2214-16 E. BROAD ST. 2
*1845 to 1850*

These three double mid-century houses have suffered superficial changes, including the various porch additions. They would create a fine effect if restored.

2300 E. BROAD STREET 3
*1850*

The exterior of this fine Greek Revival house has been restored to its original appearance in the course of adapting it for use as a private club and apartments.

Carrington Square

The block just west of St. John's Church between Broad and Grace and extending from Twenty-third to Twenty-fourth Street is made up of houses built between 1810 and 1890. It was selected as the pilot restoration block for the Church Hill area, and was named for the Carrington family, several members of which built homes here. The development of the landscaped mews through the center was carried out by the Garden Club of Virginia; it retains the old cobblestone alley and incorporates examples of Richmond ironwork.

2305 E. BROAD STREET                          4
*1854*

This mid-nineteenth-century dwelling has been renovated
for contemporary use but not "restored" in the sense
of removing the alterations of a later period (c. 1916).
The square attic windows are characteristic of its date;
however, the window brows, the diamond-paned sash,
and the bay window are later changes. Later also is
the graceful curved porch with a tobacco leaf motif in
the column caps.

CARRINGTON ROW                                5
*2307-11 E. Broad Street*
*1818*

This magnificent row of connected houses is unique for
its period in Richmond, and is the earliest row now remaining. The recessed panels, elliptical fanlights, and

pilasters on the front façade are interesting features. The restoration made in 1965 by the Historic Richmond Foundation honors the alterations previously made in the entranceway treatments, each reflecting a different period and style: Greek Revival, Federal, and Victorian.

HARDGROVE HOUSE 6
*2300 E. Grace Street*
*1849*

This stately Greek Revival residence was built by a tobacco manufacturer. The original two-story servants' quarters are still standing in rear. Another outbuilding in the rear yard may antedate the main house and is said to have been used in early tobacco manufacturing experiments. The house was restored in 1960-61 by the Historic Richmond Foundation.

HILARY BAKER HOUSE                          7
*2302 E. Grace Street*
*before 1816*


ANN CARRINGTON HOUSE                        8
*2306 E. Grace Street*
*between 1810 and 1816*

These two houses are fine examples of the Federal
style. Both have Flemish bond brickwork, large double
chimneys, and plaster keystone window lintels. The
porch at 2302 was added when the house was restored
and its style is associated with a slightly later period.
The bow front at 2306 is unusual in Richmond.

   The Ann Carrington house served as the rectory of
St. John's during the early part of the present century.
Both houses are now owned by the Association for the

Preservation of Virginia Antiquities and were restored by its William Byrd Branch.

HARWOOD AND ESTES HOUSES  9
*2308 and 2310 E. Grace Street*
*1869*

These similar houses, built the same year, contribute the charm of a later period to the pilot restoration block. The fine cast-iron verandas are typical of many made in local foundries.

2312-14 AND 2316 E. GRACE STREET          10
*1885*

This double house and the detached dwelling on the corner do not equal their neighbors to the east in architectural quality; they date from an era when artistic taste had declined. However, they serve to complete a harmonious block façade which exhibits a full array of nineteenth-century design, with the individual houses dating from 1810 to 1885. The corner house, 2316, was the home of John Garland Pollard, a governor of Virginia.

WHITLOCK HOUSE          11
*316 N. 24th Street*
*1840*

This house is covered with beaded siding, usually associated with an earlier period. It has been restored and is used as a crafts shop.

*St. John's Church, with steeple of 1866-96*

## ST. JOHN'S CHURCH 12

*E. Broad Street between 24th and 25th*

*1741*

St. John's Church has a large place in history. The Virginia Convention met here in 1775, with Washington, Jefferson, and other founding fathers present, and voted to arm the colony against the British Crown. This was the occasion of Patrick Henry's famous speech ending, "Is life so dear, or peace so sweet as to be purchased at the price of chains and slavery? Forbid it, Almighty God. I know not what course others may take, but as for me, give me liberty or give me death!"

The original part of this church, the present transept, is considered to be the oldest building in the city. It was first enlarged in 1772; the belfry was erected in 1830 and has been replaced twice. Two small accessory buildings are of interest: the brick Sunday school built in the 1830's and the tiny frame vestry room in Gothic style.

The architectural value of St. John's is more than just its venerable age: its setting makes it a landmark amid the serenity of its old burial ground.

2403

2407

2403 AND 2407 E. GRACE STREET                    13
*1844*

These two houses were built by Mrs. John Van Lew, whose
mansion stood in the next block to the west and was torn
down to make way for the Bellevue School. Built as a
real estate investment, the houses were probably identical
originally. 2403 retains its original Greek portico but
has had embellishments made to the cornice and window
heads; both porch and cornice of 2407 have been remodeled. The latter is known as the Elmira Shelton
house; Poe visited here shortly before his death. It is
now the headquarters of the Historic Richmond Foundation.

ST. PATRICK'S CHURCH 14
*215 N. 25th Street*
*1859*

Interesting as a period piece rather than as outstanding architecture, this Roman Catholic church shows the Gothic Revival influence which dominated the design of religious building during the latter half of the nineteenth century.

*2500 E. Grace*

*207 N. 25th Street*

## JOHN MORRIS COTTAGES                                  15
*2500 E. Grace Street and 207 N. 25th Street*
*1830 and 1835*

These two frame cottages survive from a period when few houses were built in Richmond. They have been beautifully restored by the Historic Richmond Foundation. The corner house is the older of the two.

ADAMS DOUBLE HOUSE 16
*2501-3 E. Grace Street*
*1809-10*

Dating from an early stage of development on Church
Hill, this is a typical double house of its period. The
present entrance porches were added when the street
grade was lowered (c. 1880), and a store front has been
inserted on the end. Dr. John Adams, who built this
house, had extensive real estate holdings on the hill and
initiated development in the area. This valuable part
of the city's architectural heritage is being restored by
Historic Richmond Foundation in memory of Wyndham
B. Blanton, its first president.

2517 AND 2519 E. GRACE STREET          17
*1857 and 1862*

These two restored houses show characteristics of
Richmond dwellings around 1860: nearly flat roofs,
living room windows starting at the floor, and the slim
styling of the porches. The more elaborate of these
houses, at 2519, is one of a very few residences built in
Richmond during the Civil War; the window head trim
is of iron.

ANDREW ELLETT HOUSE          18
*2702 E. Grace Street*
*1829*

A good example of the period before the Greek Revival
style became predominant in Richmond, this is a handsome house, and valuable to the city because not many
dwellings are left from this time. It should be restored.

WHITE-TAYLOR HOUSE 19
*2717 E. Grace Street*
*1839*

This large house is an architectural composite since it retains its classical portico but underwent alterations about 1880, when the third story was added. The cast-iron window pediments and veranda are from the later date. The carriage house was built at the same time as the original house.

BODEKER HOUSE 20
*2801 E. Grace Street*
*1852*

This good Greek Revival house, with a Doric portico on granite base and steps, has been handsomely restored.

2800-2802 E. GRACE STREET                    21
*1862*

This double house, recently renovated, has characteristics
of an earlier period in the steep roof and the stepped
parapets of the end walls.

215 AND 217 N. 28TH STREET                  22
*1852 and 1858*

Two similar diminutive houses which are next-door
neighbors, these are attractive in their simplicity; 217 has
recently been renovated.

WILLIAMSON ALLEN HOUSE                    23
*107 N. 29th Street*
*1857*

This is typical of the frame houses built by people of modest means in the mid-nineteenth century.

## Libby Hill

Libby Hill is a spur of Church Hill, with steep bluffs on its east and south faces. It commands a panoramic view southward, down and across the James. The park here is one of four created by the City Council in 1851.

Although there were houses on Libby Hill before 1800, the oldest now standing, 2718 E. Franklin Street, was built in 1839. The rows of dwellings which frame two sides of the park were mostly built during the latter half of the nineteenth century. The block of Twenty-ninth Street along the east side has large houses at each end which were built in 1850; the dwellings between are from later decades. Richmond ornamental ironwork at its best may be seen in the veranda of the Hancock house, 11½ N. Twenty-ninth Street, built in 1868; the houses south of it display typical ironwork of the next

two decades. Wood scroll-saw porches, characteristic of the same period, adorn the houses facing the park on Franklin.

HANCOCK HOUSE                                24
*11½ N. 29th Street*
*1868*

LUTHER LIBBY HOUSE                    25
*1 N. 29th Street*
*1850*

The original gable roof has been replaced by a mansard one. Libby rented a warehouse at the Richmond Dock; taken over during the Civil War, it became notorious as "Libby Prison."

CONFEDERATE SOLDIERS AND
SAILORS MONUMENT                    26
*1894*
*sculptor: William Ludwell Sheppard*

A bronze figure which stands on a granite shaft modeled on Pompey's Column in Rome, this memorial is a prominent landmark because of its height and situation on the axis of Main Street. The sculptor was a prominent Richmond artist.

3017-19 LIBBY TERRACE                                    27
*1857*

This frame double house has a beautiful site on the eastern brow of Libby Hill.

3017 WILLIAMSBURG AVENUE                        28
*1799-1802*

This house is outside the Church Hill district at the base of Libby Hill. The third oldest frame dwelling remaining in Richmond, it stands in a poor neighborhood and is in need of repair. It was built by a sea captain close to Rocketts, then the port of Richmond.

2718 E. FRANKLIN STREET 29

*1839*

Originally one story high, this house has had several additions including the interesting cupola. The servants' house in the rear, of an early date, is notable.

2600 AND 2602 E. FRANKLIN STREET 30

*1855 and 1856*

2617 E. FRANKLIN STREET                                    31
*1856*

2611 E. FRANKLIN STREET                                    32
*1857*

These four Greek Revival houses of the mid-fifties have
all been restored recently, attesting to the renascence of
Church Hill as a present-day residential neighborhood.

## 2601 AND 2603-5 E. FRANKLIN STREET 33
*1857 and 1858*

Of these two late Greek Revival houses, one has had
a third story added; the other has been extended to the
east, placing the Ionic portico entrance in the center.
The houses are joined by a curious filler of a later date.

## ANTHONY TURNER HOUSE 34
*2520 E. Franklin Street*
*between 1803 and 1810*

This is a handsome survival of early nineteenth-century
domestic architecture. The window heads were changed
in front and the second-story ones have not been restored;
elsewhere there are stone lintels, some original and some
replaced.

316 N. 27TH STREET                                    35
*before 1814*

This is one of the oldest houses on Church Hill; the
porch and window lintels are later changes.

2606 E. MARSHALL STREET                              36
*1814*

An early nineteenth-century dwelling with a steep gable
roof that is characteristic of the period, this house is
worthy of restoration.

WILLS' STORE 37
*401 N. 27th Street*
*1813-15*

Built as a grocery store, this is thought to be the oldest
shop now standing in Richmond.

405 N. 27TH STREET 38
*1835*

The delicate cornice, simple but graceful porch, and
triple windows make this restored house interesting.

407 N. 27TH STREET                              39
*1812 or earlier*

If restored to its original condition, this would be a
unique dwelling type on the Richmond scene. It was
a mansion with lower wings on each side of the central
mass. The north wing has been completely altered, and
is used as a separate house. This alteration, as well as
the porch addition, the changed window sash, and the
asphalt covering, all combine to denigrate its past.
Charles Wills, who built this house, also built the store
at 401 N. Twenty-seventh Street.

501 N. 27TH STREET                              40
*before 1819*

This is one of the oldest buildings surviving in Shed
Town. The porch and rear wing are later additions.

## 509 N. 27TH STREET 41
*1817-18*

The belt course and window head treatment are characteristic of the period. The porch is probably of a later date, as are the window sash and entrance door.

## 510 N. 29TH STREET 42
*between 1816 and 1820*

This house has been recently repaired. Unfortunately the new porch hides the recessed panels, which are typical decorative elements of the period. The steep gable, Flemish bond brickwork, and cornice remain to testify to its age.

LEIGH STREET BAPTIST CHURCH          43
*E. Leigh Street at 25th Street*
*1853*
*architect: Samuel Sloan*

This is a magnificent example of the use of the Greek
temple form in church architecture. The cast-iron railings are an enhancement.


## Union Hill and Shed Town

These are the names of nineteenth-century settlements
north of Church Hill. Union and Church Hills are
topographically distinct, although the ravine which once
lay between them has been partially filled and graded
to make Jefferson Avenue. Like Church Hill, Union
Hill has a steep western bluff above Shockoe Valley.
Shed Town refers to a community with more ambiguous

boundaries, a plateau merging with Union Hill roughly along Twenty-fifth Street and with Church Hill along M Street. The area contains many dwellings built prior to the Civil War, modest homes built by tradesmen and working people; many of these are now in rather poor condition. This section has seen a racial shift from white to Negro occupancy. It is interesting to note, however, that before the Civil War free Negroes built homes here in a white working-class neighborhood, unhindered by prejudice or pattern of segregation.

The Union Hill settlement was developed with an irregular street network in order to cope with the steep terrain; it is largely to this that it owes its extraordinary picturesque character.

618 AND 620 N. 27TH STREET
*1843 and 1847*

These two Greek Revival houses, almost identical, were built as homes of small tradesmen.

SPRINGFIELD HALL
*700 N. 26th Street*
*c. 1852 (demolished 1976)*

Built as headquarters of the Springfield Lodge, Sons of Temperance, this is now a church.

821 N. 23RD STREET
*1849*

Here is a basically unaltered example of a workman's or tradesman's house, now in its second century of use.

## 2121 VENABLE STREET
*1854*

Shown here is a dwelling type that is rare in Richmond, the so-called "raised cottage." There is another quite similar, built three years later, at 601 N. Thirtieth Street.

## Capitol Square

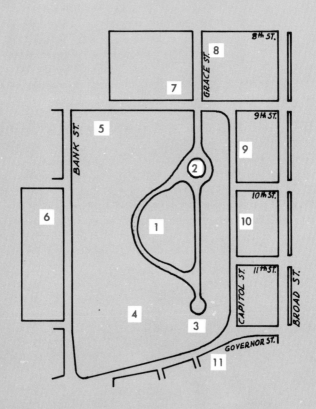

## Capitol Square

The government center of the new state was moved to Richmond from Williamsburg in 1779. The legislature convened in temporary quarters and the following year selected Shockoe Hill as the site for the Capitol. When

*Capitol Square ca. 1856-58*

the new Capitol was opened for use in 1788, it commanded a panoramic view of the river valley: the terrain was open over a vast sweeping slope south to the James River. Early prints show how the Capitol once dominated the city skyline (see pp. 25, 27).

Today the river is mostly sealed off from view, and the Capitol itself is not visible from any considerable distance because tall buildings have gone up in the neighboring blocks. It does, however, hold reign over its own green square, a park setting allotted to it when the site was first chosen. The square was for many years an unkempt wasteland, ungraded and crossed by gullies. In 1816 Maximilian Godefroy, a French architect who had been exiled by Napoleon, was called to Richmond to renovate the Capitol and make a landscape plan for the square. His plan was a formal one

in the French tradition. At mid-century, a prominent
Philadelphia architect, John Notman, was commissioned
to redesign the grounds; he did so in the romantic style
that had become fashionable, and that is the image that
remains today.

Capitol Square has in and around it an array of
valuable buildings from Richmond's nineteenth-century
past, although the Capitol itself is the only one remaining from the century before. Within the square are
the Governor's Mansion (1812), an unusual architectural
feature in the form of a bell tower (1824), and the
Washington Monument, unveiled in 1858. The tower
and the monument are positioned on the axes of Franklin
and Grace Streets respectively, and thus effectively
relate the square to the streets outside.

Significant buildings along Capitol Street, which
borders the square on the north, include the City Hall, a
rugged Victorian period piece (1887-94), and the new
Life of Virginia office building, one of Richmond's
handsomer contemporary structures. Closing the view
at the east end of Capitol Street is a Victorian row house
(1853), a unique survival in the city. South of Capitol
Square, on Bank Street, the main post office building
is an extension of the earlier Custom House (1859).
West of the square, on Grace Street, are two distinguished
nineteenth-century churches: historic St. Paul's (1845)
on the corner of Ninth Street and St. Peter's (1834), a
block west at Eighth Street.

These then are Capitol Square's landmarks of the
past; what of the future? Obviously the needs of the
state government for administrative space have increased
enormously. The response to this at first was not very
farsighted: witness the crowding in on the southeast
corner of the square of two tall state office buildings, one
now called "old," the other "new." The newer of these
is actually the beginning of a more forthright expansion
involving the rebuilding of a considerable area east of
Governor Street with a fan of high buildings swinging
around to the Virginia Department of Highways Annex
on Broad Street.

CAPITOL 1
*Capitol Square*
*1785*
*architects: Thomas Jefferson, Charles-Louis Clérisseau*

While serving as minister to France, Thomas Jefferson was asked to furnish a plan for the Virginia Capitol. He selected as a model the Roman temple known as "La Maison Carrée," built in the first century at Nîmes in southern France, and he secured the services of Charles-Louis Clérisseau, a French architect who was an authority on ancient buildings.

The cornerstone was laid in 1785 and the General Assembly met there for the first time in 1788. Jefferson's building is the central portion; the wings and the steps leading to the south portico were added in 1903-6.

The Virginia Capitol was the scene of Aaron Burr's trial for treason in 1807. In 1861 the state secession convention met here and Robert E. Lee appeared before it to accept command of the Army of Virginia. During the War between the States, the Congress of the Confederate States met here.

WASHINGTON MONUMENT                              2
*Capitol Square*
*1850-69*
*sculptor: Thomas Crawford*
*(completed by Randolph Rogers)*

Besides honoring George Washington, this monument
also commemorates six other Virginians who played a
role in the founding of the United States. The bronze
equestrian statue of Washington rests on a granite base;
around the base are six smaller statues representing
Thomas Jefferson, Patrick Henry, Andrew Lewis,
Thomas Nelson, George Mason, and John Marshall. On
a lower tier are groups of allegorical figures. Crawford
died before the work was completed; the Nelson, Mason,
and Marshall statues and the allegorical figures were
done by Rogers.


GOVERNOR'S MANSION                               3
*Capitol Square*
*1811-12*
*architect: Alexander Parris*

This has been the site of the Governor's residence since
the capital was moved to Richmond, a small frame house
having preceded this one. The first governor to live in
the present mansion was James Barbour.

The original character of the house has in general been

retained on the exterior. The wing on the east is an addition, and the enclosing brick wall replaces an earlier iron fence. The old kitchen and servants' quarters, outbuildings to the south of the main building, have been preserved.

STATE OFFICE BUILDING 4
*Capitol Square*
*1895*
*architect: W. M. Poindexter*

Built as the State Library, this neoclassic building now serves the Department of Finance.

BELL TOWER                                    5
*Capitol Square*
*1824*

The bell was used to strike the hours and sound alarms.
This tower, which replaced an earlier wooden tower
and guard house, makes an interesting focal feature at
the end of Franklin Street.


CUSTOM HOUSE                                  6
*1000 block of Bank Street*
*1858*
architects:  *Ammi B. Young and Albert Lybrock*

The original building, the central portion of the present
Post Office, was built as the U.S. Post Office and Custom
House just prior to the Civil War. It survived the
evacuation fire of 1865 which razed the blocks around it
south of Capitol Square. The subsequent extensive additions, in 1893 and 1932, have respected the character
of the original Italianate design, with two arched porticoes on Bank Street matching the original. An additional story has also been added.

   Ammi B. Young, the designer, was the first Supervis-
ing Architect of the U.S. Treasury Department; Lybrock,
a Richmond architect, was associated in some capacity,
possibly for supervision of construction.

   During the Civil War the original portion of the

building housed the Confederate Treasury Department. Later Jefferson Davis was brought here to face charges for treason; these were dismissed without trial.

ST. PAUL'S CHURCH                                    7
*E. Grace Street at 9th*
*1844-45*
*architect: Thomas S. Stewart*

A lavishly detailed church in the Classic Revival style, this was modeled on St. Luke's in Philadelphia. The original spire has been removed and replaced by a small octagonal dome. The cast-iron fence was designed by the architect. The recent addition of parish house and

connecting colonnade is a restrained and handsome asset.

Jefferson Davis and Robert E. Lee worshipped at St.
Paul's during the Civil War.

ST. PETER'S CHURCH                                    8
*E. Grace Street at 8th*
*1834*

A valuable enrichment to the downtown cityscape, this
was the cathedral of the Roman Catholic Diocese of
Richmond until 1905.

LIFE OF VIRGINIA BUILDINGS                            9
*Capitol Street*
*1912 and 1966*
*architects: Marcellus Wright and Associates*
*(new building)*

More than half a century intervened between the con-

struction of these two office buildings. Each is true to
its period and the scale of each seems just right as part
of the architectural frame around Capitol Square.

CITY HALL 10
*Capitol and Broad Streets, between 10th and 11th*
*1887-94*
*architect: Elijah E. Myers*

This massive building, made of local granite, was erected
by day labor under direction of the City Engineer. Its
predecessor as City Hall, on this site, was designed by
Robert Mills and demolished in 1874.

Valuable as a period piece and link with the past, it is
comparable with Philadelphia's City Hall and the old
State, War, and Navy building in Washington. Its
threatened destruction several years ago brought national
attention.

MORSON ROW 11
*219-23 Governor Street*
*1853*

Now used for government offices, this row of three town
houses, with bow fronts and Victorian trim, is a unique
survival in Richmond. Situated across the end of
Capitol Street, it creates a fine vista and adds interest
and variety to Capitol Square.

# North of Broad Street:
# The Medical College Area

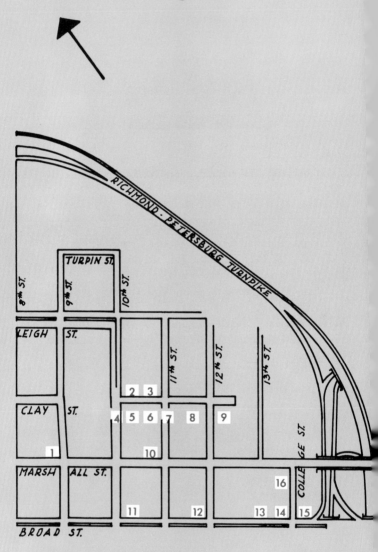

# North of Broad Street:
# The Medical College Area

Northeast from Capitol Square and across Broad Street is the Medical College of Virginia. This institution grew out of the medical department of Hampden-Sydney College, which was established in Richmond in 1838. Operating at first in rental quarters, the department built its first building in 1845, the fantastic Egyptian Building at College and Marshall Streets.

The medical center has grown enormously in recent years: its plant has gone up in the air and it has also spread out. Engulfed in this sprawling growth are a number of notable buildings, some of Richmond's most valuable heritage of architecture and history. These include, in addition to the Egyptian Building, the White House of the Confederacy, the Valentine Museum group, the Putney houses, and several churches, including Monumental Church, designed by Robert Mills. West of the Medical College, in an area the city has staked out for its civic center, stands the John Marshall house,

*The White House of the Confederacy*

historic shrine and isolated survival of eighteenth-century Richmond.

Some twelve blocks of this area, lying between Eighth and Twelfth Streets, were annexed to the town in 1780, two years before Richmond was chartered as a city. The development of this section was accelerated following the construction of the Capitol on Shockoe Hill. The growth of the Medical College has, over the past hundred years, been accommodated through rebuilding the older neighborhood and, to some extent, by the adaptation of existing buildings.

## JOHN MARSHALL HOUSE                                    1
*402 N. 9th Street*
*1788-91*

The handsomest and best preserved eighteenth-century house still standing in Richmond, this is also the only brick house surviving from its period. It was built by John Marshall, most renowned Chief Justice of the United States, and was his residence for forty-five years.

The house, which barely escaped demolition early in the present century, has been restored by the Association for the Preservation of Virginia Antiquities, and is maintained as a museum. Restoration of its grounds is in prospect.

BENJAMIN WATKINS LEIGH HOUSE 2
*1000 E. Clay Street*
*1812-16*

Contemporary with the Wickham house, across Clay Street at the other end of the block, and also built by John Wickham, this plain house has been modified by its Victorian cornice and entrance porch features. This was the home of Benjamin Watkins Leigh, U.S. Senator during the Jackson administration; later the building became a part of the Sheltering Arms Hospital.

WILLIAM H. GRANT HOUSE 3
*1008 E. Clay Street*
*1857*

This imposing mansion shows the architectural exuberance and romanticism of the 1850's. Despite conversion of the building to a hospital, the front façade is virtually unchanged. The former residence housed the Sheltering Arms Hospital from 1892 until 1965, when this charitable institution moved to modern quarters, leaving the Grant house an uncertain future.

1001 E. CLAY STREET                                    4
*1879*

This Victorian town house completes an interesting block façade of nineteenth-century houses of different periods and styles. The mansard roof and bracketed cornice were popular architectural details during the later part of the century.

BRANSFORD-CECIL MEMORIAL HOUSE          5
*1007 E. Clay Street*
*1840*

An excellent example of the Greek Revival style, this house was originally located at 13 N. Fifth Street. Later it served as church house of the Second Presbyterian Church, which was built next to it. When the church needed more space the house was dismantled and rebuilt on its present site. It now serves as an annex to the Valentine Museum.

VALENTINE MUSEUM 6
*1009-13 E. Clay Street*
*1869 or 1870*

Together with the Wickham house on the east and the
Bransford-Cecil Memorial house rebuilt adjacent to it on
the west, this building now houses the Valentine
Museum. This was a row house of three dwellings, built
as an investment by James G. Brooks, who lived at that
time in the Wickham house. Architecturally, it is a good
example of Victorian town house design: the cornice
and the bracketed pediments over the windows and doors
are typical of the time.

WICKHAM-VALENTINE HOUSE                    7
*1015 E. Clay Street*
*1812*
*architect: Robert Mills*

This house, built by John Wickham, a noted lawyer, was one of the finest of its day in Richmond. Designed by Robert Mills, who had come to Richmond at that time to design the Monumental Church, the house shares many features with the later Brockenbrough house (White House of the Confederacy), also by Mills.

The classical entrance porch, triple windows, and recessed arches are features which appear here and were frequently used thereafter in other Richmond

homes. The curved portico on the garden side and the garden itself are notable. The interiors are exceptionally fine, especially the graceful stairway.

Mann S. Valentine II bought the house in 1882; he left it, with an endowment, to be used as a museum for his varied collections. Subsequently the Valentine Museum acquired the buildings to the west; the Wickham house serves primarily to show itself, a mansion and furnishings of the early Federal period.

## MAUPIN-MAURY HOUSE          8
*1105 E. Clay Street*
*1846*

This Greek Revival house is of more interest for its historical associations than for its architecture. Its appearance has been hurt by the alteration of the entrance steps and by the change to large-pane windows.

The dwelling was built by Dr. Socrates Maupin, noted Virginia physician and educator. For a short time Matthew Fontaine Maury lived here. Commodore Maury was both naval officer and scientist; he is known as the "Pathfinder of the Seas." He is said to have experimented with models of his submarine torpedo in this house.

## WHITE HOUSE OF THE CONFEDERACY     9
*1201 E. Clay Street*
*1816-18*
*architect: Robert Mills*

Dr. John Brockenbrough, a distinguished Richmond citizen, lived in a mansion in the next block of Clay Street when he commissioned Robert Mills to design this house. It was originally a two-story residence; the third story was added in the 1850's. The house has a fine classical entrance portico and a monumental two-story veranda on the garden side.

At the time of the Civil War the building was owned by the city. It was leased by the Confederate Govern-

ment for the presidential residence, and Jefferson Davis lived here from 1861 until the evacuation in April 1865. It has served as the Confederate Museum since 1896.

PUTNEY HOUSES                                        10
*1010 and 1012 E. Marshall Street*
*1861 and 1859*

An interesting and compatible pair of town houses, originally occupied by father and son, these are now owned by the Medical College and used as dormitories. The one on the corner, the Stephen Putney house, has a striking two-story veranda of ornamental iron, the pro-

duct of a local industry, the Phoenix Iron Works. The other, which was the home of Samuel Putney, also has an ornamental iron veranda and is in the more elaborate Italianate style, exemplified by rich window trim with rounded heads and a decorative frieze as part of the cornice. These two houses are rare survivals of their period and part of an exceptionally fine block which contains the Valentine Museum group.

BROAD STREET METHODIST CHURCH          11
*E. Broad Street at 10th Street*
*1858-59    (demolished 1968)*
*architect:  Albert L. West*

This is a fine architectural period piece, a Victorian adaptation of classical motifs. Its lofty spire, once a prominent feature of the Richmond skyline, has been dismantled. The building contributes variety to the cityscape; its visual importance is increased by the way that

the City Hall is set back from Tenth Street, making the church visible from Capitol Square.

The future of the building became precarious when its congregation decided on a move toward the suburbs several years ago. How does an abandoned church attain salvation? It is expensive to adapt such buildings to other uses, and when they occupy valuable land the problem is compounded. Broad Street Methodist now belongs to the city: its use as a tourist center is under consideration.

FIRST BAPTIST CHURCH                              12
*E. Broad Street at 12th*
*1841*
*architect: Thomas U. Walter*

Like its neighbor, Broad Street Methodist in the next block west, this church building was abandoned by its congregation (in 1938), and also like its neighbor, it has fine architectural and cityscape quality. As a landmark, it gains by the reversal of scale: it is the more conspicuous because of the high buildings around it.

The church, a good example of the Greek Revival

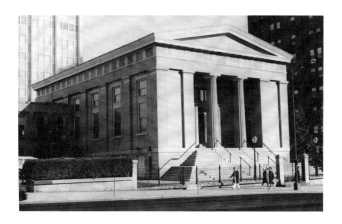

era, was designed by Thomas U. Walter, an architect of national importance, who designed the dome and wings of the U.S. Capitol.

MONUMENTAL CHURCH                                    13
*1200 block of E. Broad Street*
*1812-14*
*architect: Robert Mills*

This is one of Richmond's most notable buildings by reason of its remarkable design and the fame of its architect. Robert Mills during his long career was the creator of many public buildings in Philadelphia, Washington, Baltimore, and Charleston.

A disastrous fire razed a theater on this site in 1811. The church was begun the following year and dedicated to the memory of those who died in the fire; their names are inscribed on a monument sheltered by the massive stone portico. The main portion of the building is an octagon, covered by a dome; the architect intended to add a spire, but this was never done.

This was an Episcopal church until 1965; it is now used as the ecumenical religious center of the Medical College.

WILLIAM BEERS HOUSE                    14
*1228 E. Broad Street*
*1839*

Originally built two stories high on a raised basement, with a gable roof, this house had a third story and the present cornice added in 1860. The Greek portico entrance and wrought-iron handrail are noteworthy. The building has been successfully adapted to office use.

## FIRST AFRICAN BAPTIST CHURCH 15
*College Street at E. Broad Street*
*1876*

The original First Baptist Church was built on this site in 1803. When a new church was built up the hill at Broad and Twelfth in 1841, the Negro part of the congregation stayed on in the old location and later replaced the old building with the one standing here now.

Originally it was stuccoed and had a cupola. The Greek design echoes a period earlier than the seventies and may well have been inspired by the Thomas U. Walter church of 1841. The building has been altered by the Medical College for classroom use.

## EGYPTIAN BUILDING 16
*E. Marshall and College Streets*
*1845*
*architect: Thomas S. Stewart*

This unique building is a radical departure from the Greek Revival style which dominated architectural design in America during the decade of the 1840's. Only a year before, the same architect had designed St. Paul's Church on Grace Street at Capitol Square along classical lines. The architect detailed the iron fence here, as he did for St. Paul's. The Egyptian decor of the building

is echoed in the fence, which has posts in the form of mummy cases.

Hampden-Sydney College established a medical department in Richmond in 1838, occupying at that time the old Union Hotel at Nineteenth and Main Streets. The need for a new building, and appropriations from the city and the state legislature, resulted in the purchase of this site and the commissioning of the Egyptian Building. The medical department was later chartered as the Medical College of Virginia, which still uses this, the oldest medical college building in the South.

# North of Broad Street:
# Jackson Ward

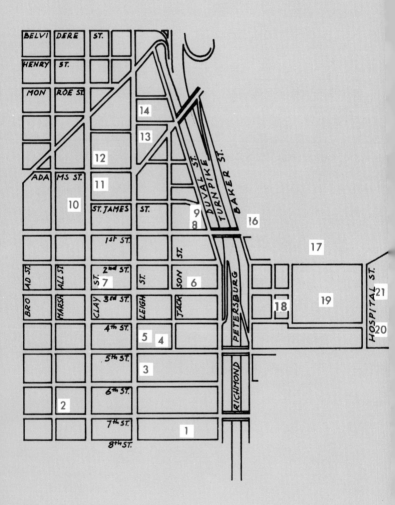

# North of Broad Street:
# Jackson Ward

The name "Jackson Ward" no longer refers to a political district, but has traditionally been used to connote an area north of Broad Street, long the largest Negro residential neighborhood in Richmond. For the purpose of this architectural description this neighborhood will be considered as extending north from Broad Street and west from Eighth Street, going across the Petersburg Turnpike to include the area around Shockoe Cemetery, and west across Belvidere for several blocks along Clay, Catherine, and Leigh Streets.

A sizable part of this area was annexed to the city in 1793; further additions were made in 1810. As late as 1950 nearly half of the pre-Civil War houses still standing in Richmond were to be found in this section of the city. However, recent traffic planning has cut the area into pieces, first with the Belvidere widening crossing north to south, and then with the turnpike taking out a great block-wide swathe. Further street widenings and interchanges are in prospect. Moreover, commercial transition has been taking over the part closest to downtown, and the demolition of several blocks is planned to make a site for a coliseum and convention center.

Despite these forces of change, and despite the rundown condition of much of this large neighborhood, there still remains something worth seeing in the way of nineteenth-century houses and block-long swatches of pleasant urban cityscape. If the ultimate city-planning decisions permit the retention of some of this as residential environment then there is much to be gained through preservation and rehabilitation of the dwellings. The rationale for this is quite simple: many of these blocks of nineteenth-century houses could, through restoration, be made into an urban domestic setting far superior to the kind of new project housing that is currently being built.

RICHMOND HOWITZERS ARMORY                    1
*600 block of N. 8th Street*
*1895*

Here is the turreted splendor of late 19th century romantic military architecture. No longer in use, the building is in the path of the Medical College expansion.

THE BLUES ARMORY                              2
*E. Marshall and 6th Streets*
*1909*

The corbeled towers and sidewalk arcades contribute picturesque variety to the downtown scene. This armory was the headquarters for the Richmond Light Infantry Blues until 1965. The ground floor serves as a city market.

HAWES HOUSE                                              3
*506 E. Leigh Street*
*1816 (demolished 1968)*

Last occupied as a residence in 1875, this building has
subsequently been used for an orphanage, a club, and
Salvation Army Headquarters. Removal of the entrance
porch, rearrangement of front steps, and inappropriate
shutters are unfortunate alterations that detract from
the appearance.

608-10 N. FIFTH STREET                                   4
*1833 (probably) (demolished)*

This well-proportioned house was divided into two dwellings in the 1850's. The cornice is a later addition.

410 E. LEIGH STREET                                    5
*c. 1870   (demolished)*

Ornamental iron verandas were common enhancements
of even modest homes in Richmond during the two
decades following the Civil War. This is a choice survival.

612 N. THIRD STREET                                    6
*1800 or 1801*

The gambrel-roofed, or "Dutch," cottage was a domestic
style used in Virginia from colonial days up to the beginning of the nineteenth century. Here is one of two
which survive in Richmond today. There was a large
chimney on the end away from the street; this was taken
down when the cinder-block extension was made.

204 E. CLAY STREET 7
*1848*

This is a well-maintained example of Greek Revival domestic architecture of the mid-nineteenth century.

23-25 E. DUVAL STREET 8
*1815-17*

This double house is one of the oldest structures in this neighborhood. The molded brick cornice and stucco-surfaced window lintels are characteristic of its period.

19 E. DUVAL STREET                               9
*1818-19   (demolished)*

One of the oldest houses in this neighborhood, this has
been altered by addition of porch and replacement of
original window sash.

ADDOLPH DILL HOUSE                              10
*oo Clay Street*
*1832*

This is valuable as the only mansion remaining from its
time, for very few houses were built in Richmond during
the 1820's and 30's. Notable features are the handsome
cornice, entrance porch with marble steps, and interior
palette-shaped staircase. Since 1922 this house has been
used as a club and more recently as a public library.

FIRST BLOCK OF W. CLAY STREET                    11
*mid-19th century*

West Clay Street, from the Addolph Dill house at 00 west to Belvidere Street, presents an array of nineteenth-century dwellings. These five or six blocks have remarkably good unity and domestic scale. There is a concentration of mid-century houses in the first block, between St. James and Adams Streets. The houses at 8, 10, 12, and 14 were built between 1847 and 1855. The church

at the corner of Adams Street dates from 1859 but has had a façade, in the 1890 version of Gothic, applied to it. Across the street at 15 and 21 are two houses built by Addolph Dill in 1846 and 1847.

106 TO 114 W. CLAY STREET        12
*c. 1875*

An attractive street picture is made by this group of Victorian houses, enhanced by the ornamental ironwork of the verandas.

FIRST BATTALION ARMORY 13
*W. Leigh and St. Peter Streets*
*1895*

Here is another "fairy tale" armory from the nineties
with characteristic decorative terra-cotta and stone trim.

EBENEZER BAPTIST CHURCH 14
*W. Leigh and Judah Streets*
*1873*

This curious design resulted from the alteration of an
earlier frame church built in 1858.

815 W. CLAY STREET                          15
*1859*

The long windows on the front porch and the low, almost
flat, roof are characteristic features of dwellings built just
prior to the Civil War.

909 ST. JAMES STREET                        16
*1845*

This frame house of the mid-1840's retains its original
appearance.

1115 N. 1ST STREET                    17
*1816 (probably) (demolished)*

The raised appearance of this house, one of the oldest standing in this neighborhood, results from a past lowering of the street grade. The entrance porch, though probably a later addition, is appropriate.

1013 N. 3RD STREET                    18
*1790*

Valuable as representing a period dwelling that is all but extinct in Richmond, this is one of two eighteenth-century gambrel-roofed cottages. The changes to this one, such as the asphalt roll siding, are rather superficial and restoration should be possible. This cottage was moved here in 1875 from its original location at Fourth and Marshall Streets.

SHOCKOE CEMETERY                                   19

This is the burial ground where many Richmond citizens, prominent ones as well as common folk, were interred between the years of 1825 and 1875. With its fine trees and handsome iron fences it is a place of calm and beauty.

Chief Justice John Marshall is buried here, with his wife and daughter. Others whose names are prominent in Richmond history include: John Wickham; Claudius Crozet; Elmira Shelton and Jane Craig Stanard, both remembered because of Edgar Allan Poe; and Elizabeth Van Lew, whose efforts for the Union cause are legendary.

HEBREW CEMETERY                                    20
*Hospital Street at 5th Street*

This cemetery, across Hospital Street from the northeast corner of historic Shockoe Cemetery, occupies a dramatic site on a bluff above Shockoe Valley. It was

opened in 1816. Of particular note is the Confederate section, marked by a striking cast-iron fence of stacked rifles and crossed sabres.

RICHMOND NURSING HOME 21
*Hospital Street facing Shockoe Cemetery*
*1860*

Built by the city as an alms house, this building served as a Confederate hospital during the Civil War.

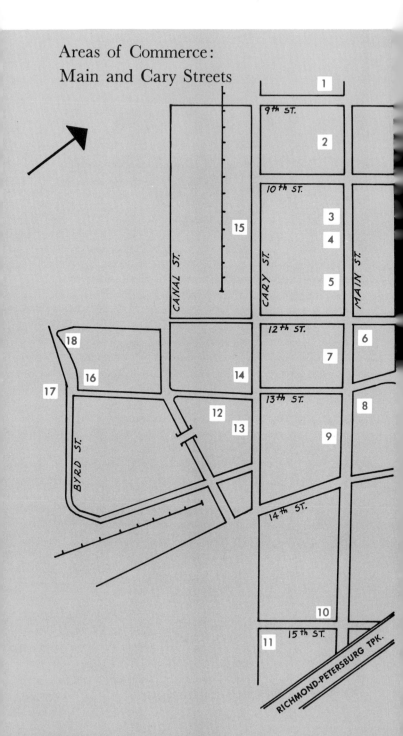

Areas of Commerce:
Main and Cary Streets

## Areas of Commerce:
## Main and Cary Streets

The business center of the town grew to the west. The location of the Capitol on Shockoe Hill, the residential section that grew around it, the bridge across the James at Fourteenth—these factors all operated to pull the chief trading area of the growing city over to the west side of Shockoe Creek and up the hill along Main Street before the eighteenth century had ended.

These blocks of Main Street were lined with a mixture of houses, stores, taverns, and inns in the early part of the nineteenth century. But commercial obsolescence came quickly and there was much change and rebuilding, with the early inns disappearing before the Civil War. Whatever was there then was largely swept away by the evacuation fire of 1865.

A fortuitous result of the fire was that Richmond had an abundance of commercial architecture created in the brief period of cast-iron construction. This mate-

ESTABLISHED 1851. INCORPORATED 1871.

Business transferred from buildings corner Cary and 10th Sts. to new buildings corner 25th and Main Sts. July 1st 1876.

Salesroom 1400 Main Street

RICHMOND STOVE WORKS
RICHMOND, VA.

rial provided the supporting skeleton of the buildings and
also the sheathing of the façades. The rich adornment
produced by the foundries, drawing usually on classical
decorative features, resulted in a variety of machine-
made works of art.

Several blocks of lower Main and Cary Streets stayed
almost intact into the middle of the twentieth century.
The long survival of these buildings has also been fortuitous; by the time of the First World War the center of
downtown had moved up to Grace Street, and although
banks and office buildings were built on Main Street,
the lower blocks of the street were relatively stagnant.
Thus the older buildings, or many of them, remained.

Attrition, however, has accelerated in the 1960's:
these buildings, with upper stories unused, have been
coming down. Below Tenth Street, the tendency is to
replace them with lower buildings, more utilitarian and

*James River & Kanawha Canal, packet office at 8th Street*

efficient, but less handsome. Or else the land is used,
temporarily, as a parking lot, leaving a gaping hole in the
street façade.

The land between Cary Street and the James is of
interest more for what used to be than for what is there
now. From the corner of Twelfth and Cary Streets one

can look south to Basin-Bank Street; this raised roadway
formed the north bank of the turning basin in the canal
days. The basin, which was the terminal of the James
River and Kanawha Canal, was connected to the Richmond Dock through a series of six locks. Remains of two
of these may still be seen between Byrd and Canal Streets.
The ashlar stonework is exceptionally fine masonry.
These should be preserved and restored.

FIRST NATIONAL BANK                                    1
*E. Main and 9th Streets, southwest corner*
*1912*

The American derivation of the Paris Beaux-Arts design
school dominated commercial and public architecture
over the first three decades of the twentieth century. This
bank and office building is characteristic: the skeleton-
frame building is faced with classical ornament in stone,
from the monumental columns at the base to the cornice
at the top.

911-13 E. MAIN STREET                              2
*c. 1870*

This decorative building with iron window trim and
bracket cornice is characteristic of its period. At street
level the fronts have been remodeled: the one at 911
retains the cast iron and respects the original design with
most effective results.

1007-13 E. MAIN STREET                             3
*c. 1866*

A superb cast-iron row built just after the Civil War,
with ironwork by Hayward, Bartlett of Baltimore. The
street-level alterations vary greatly in quality. The front
at 1011 is a tasteless desecration of the building's char-

acter, whereas the one at 1007, though contemporary
in feeling, respects the original design and is quite handsome. This building is a rare survival and every effort
should be made to preserve it.

1015 E. MAIN STREET 4
*c. 1866*

Another fine survival of the Civil War decade, this building retains its original façade unchanged. The treatment
at ground-floor level is noteworthy, with its classical
colonnade and recessed entrances.

1109, 1111, AND 1113 E. MAIN STREET          5
*c. 1866 and later   (demolished 1971)*

Of these three commercial buildings with cast-iron fronts
at the street floor, the central one is probably of a later
date than the other two.  1109 has an especially handsome façade at the lower level; unfortunately the western
half of this building has been demolished.

1200 E. MAIN STREET                                    6
*1893*

Richmond formerly had a number of commercial buildings in the Romanesque Revival style which was made
popular by the work of H. H. Richardson. This building, built for the Planters National Bank, is the only one
remaining.

1207-11 E. MAIN STREET                                 7
*1866*

This is one of two commercial row buildings with full
cast-iron fronts now standing on Main Street. Like the
one at 1007-13, it was built shortly after this area was
leveled by the evacuation fire. This row surpasses the
other in the ornateness of its iron work: it is a foundry-
produced Italian palace. The remodeling at 1209, done

in 1966, is an insensitive desecration. The building as a whole is a rare representative of its era, contributing variety and identity to the Richmond cityscape.

1300 TO 1310 E. MAIN STREET                8
*c. 1870-80  (demolished)*

This is a characteristic and interesting group of commercial buildings.  1306 has a full cast-iron façade, with engaged columns and balustrades.

1321 AND 1321½ E. MAIN STREET                9
*c. 1870*

These buildings display a variety of cast-iron work. The curious one at 1321½ is only eight-and-a-half feet wide.

## 1441 AND 1443 E. MAIN STREET 10
*1813-14  (demolished)*

The evacuation fire razed the south side of Main Street from Ninth Street down to these buildings. Originally stores with dwellings above, these are the oldest structures along this part of Main Street. Time and alterations have treated both in unkindly fashion; the gable and dormer have been removed from 1443.

## WORTHAM AND McGRUDER WAREHOUSE 11
*27 S. 15th Street*
*1830  (demolished)*

This building is of interest as one of the oldest commercial buildings standing in Richmond. Noteworthy features are the delicate wood trim around the windows, the picturesque loft window, and the brickwork in Flemish bond pattern.

SHOCKOE SLIP                                          12
*E. Cary at 13th Street*

This picturesque little piazza, surrounded by warehouses
and used partially as a loading area for trucks, is potentially a fine urban space. Destruction of a building on
the south side for a parking lot has removed one wall
of the space; a building is needed here for enclosure.

The focal point of Shockoe Slip is the granite fountain, placed there for the watering of draught horses.
The texture of the cobbled floor, the classical iron-frame
doorway of the old Grain Exchange, and the Revolutionary War cannon used as a bollard on the corner are
features which contribute to the visual quality of this
court.

WATERING FOUNTAIN
*Shockoe Slip*
*1909*

Replacing an earlier fountain, this delightful piece of
street furniture is dedicated to Capt. Charles S. Morgan,
C.S.A., "in memory of one who loved animals."

COLUMBIAN BLOCK 13
*1301-7 E. Cary Street*
*1871*

This building served as the Richmond Grain and Cotton Exchange. It stands on the site of the Columbian Hotel, which was destroyed in the 1865 fire.

E. CARY STREET 14
*1200 and 1300 blocks*
*c. 1870-80*

The blocks on Cary Street east and west of Shockoe Slip have an extraordinary visual quality. The buildings that line the sides are mostly warehouses and wholesale places. Plainer than the iron façades on Main Street, these are mostly of unadorned brick with cast-iron store fronts at the street level only. The commercial row at 1211-19 is especially notable.

WAREHOUSE                                              15
*1019-21 E. Cary Street*
*mid-19th century  (demolished)*

This building was originally a warehouse for water-transported goods; it faced on the turning basin of the canal. It has a handsome store front of granite on the Cary Street side. Another warehouse of similar vintage, with stepped gable ends and Flemish bond brickwork, stood in the next block east until it was partially burned and demolished in 1967.

CANAL LOCKS                                            16
*Byrd Street between 12th and 13th Streets*
*after 1840*

This block-long channel between granite walls is all that remains visible in central Richmond of a canal system that was in its day of great importance to the city's commerce.

The remnant here, displaying fine masonry work, is a portion of the works built by the James River and Kanawha Company to connect the main turning basin (bounded by Eighth, Basin-Bank, Twelfth, and Canal

Streets) with the Richmond Dock. The exposed part here, between Twelfth and Thirteenth Streets, contained two locks; two other locks are now buried beneath a parking lot to the west.

MILL FOUNDATIONS 17
*E. Byrd Street at 13th Street*

The date of these foundations is not known. They are on land which was once owned by the Haxall and Crenshaw Company and are presumed to have been a part of their flour milling operations. Haxall's mills were built on the spot of the first grist mill at the river falls, and were thrice destroyed by fire, in 1830, 1865, and 1874. One of the mill buildings still stands close by at Byrd and Twelfth Streets.

These foundation walls, nearly eight feet thick, must have supported a structure of considerable height.

HAXALL MILL BUILDING 18
*E. Byrd Street at 12th*
*mid-19th century (demolished)*

Here is the lone survival of a flour milling enterprise that was of great economic importance to Richmond throughout most of the nineteenth century. The date of this building is uncertain; it is possibly as late as 1872, or it may have been built before the Civil War.

# Capitol Square to Monroe Park

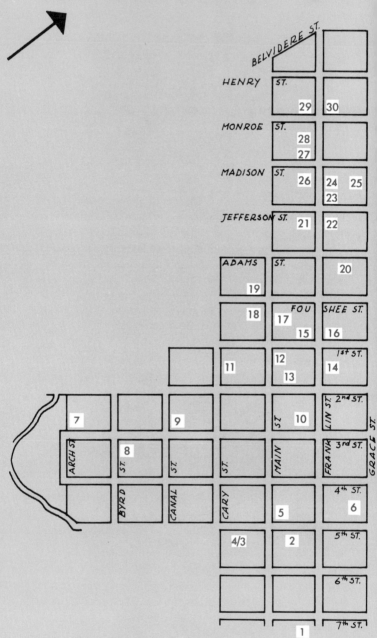

# Capitol Square to Monroe Park

From Capitol Square west to Monroe Park, the area south of Broad Street has been very largely rebuilt in the twentieth century. At the beginning of the century the city's finest residential streets were to be found here; now only fragments are left.

The southern terminus of Third and Fourth Streets is on Gamble's Hill, a bluff overlooking the James and the industrial panorama along it. This eminence was the site of a mansion built in 1798-99 to the design of Benjamin Latrobe, the most noted architect of the early republic. Although this house did not last out the nineteenth century, Gamble's Hill became in time a fine residential neighborhood and had as recently as twenty years ago potential for revival as a good in-town place of residence. That potential is no more; the transition to commercial use is virtually complete. A few old dwellings still stand on Third Street, all by virtue of being remodeled as offices.

The story of Grace and Franklin Streets, and also Main and Cary, and the blocks between them, is much the same. Grace Street was once the social center of Richmond; since World War I it has become instead the retail center, and today it retains no trace of its former character. The transition of Franklin Street came somewhat later, and a portion of it yet holds some of its earlier domestic quality. Of the entire area from Capitol Square west to Monroe Park between Broad and the river, only those seven blocks of Franklin Street from First Street west were, by 1966, classed in a residential category on the city's zoning map. But even here transformation to a new and more intensive residential use in the form of tall apartment buildings is plainly visible. Until recently the Jefferson Hotel was the soaring landmark on a street built otherwise at domestic scale. Now several tall buildings surround it. For the moment there is a lively contrast between the old scale and the new on Franklin Street, and it makes for interesting cityscape. However, if the rebuilding trend continues and the older buildings give way entirely, then a fine urban street will have succumbed to monotony.

NORMAN STEWART HOUSE                    1
*707 E. Franklin Street*
*1844*

This simple well-proportioned example of the Greek Revival style is a lone domestic survival of a residential neighborhood which has otherwise completely vanished. It was rented by General Lee's family in the final war years, and Lee lived here for two months following Appomattox. It is now owned by the Confederate Memorial Literary Society.

SECOND PRESBYTERIAN CHURCH 2

*N. 5th between Main and Franklin*

*1847*

*architect: Minard Lafever*

An important part of Richmond's architectural heritage, this church building was the first local adaptation of the Gothic Revival style of the middle years of the century. The brick was originally painted gray. Stonewall Jackson worshipped here when in Richmond.

The connecting church house is an addition of recent years. Fortunately, the Bransford house, a good residence of the Greek Revival period which it replaced, has been preserved, having been rebuilt on Clay Street as part of the Valentine Museum.

SCOTT-CLARKE HOUSE                                    3
*9 S. 5th Street*
*1841*

BARRET HOUSE                                          4
*13 S. 5th Street*
*1844*

These two superb dwellings have survived the passing of
their neighborhood through adaptation to office use.
Actually the quality of the design makes a distinguished
business headquarters. The Barret house has been called
"the high point of Classic Revival architecture in Richmond."

HANCOCK-CASKIE HOUSE       5
*2 N. 5th Street*
*1808-9*

Of outstanding architectural importance, this mansion is a survival from the first decade of the nineteenth century, and its octagonal form is unique today in Richmond.

For a time the home of William Wirt, Attorney General of the United States, this house has been successfully adapted for office use.

CENTENARY METHODIST CHURCH       6
*E. Grace between 4th and 5th Streets*
*1845*
*architects: John and Samuel Freeman*

The Gothic Revival tower and façade of this church are the result of a remodeling in 1874 by Albert L. West, architect of Broad Street and Trinity Methodist Churches.

322 S. 3RD STREET     7
*1861 (demolished)*

This simple house is another example of preservation through remodeling for present-day use. The ornamental ironwork on veranda and balcony, probably contemporary with the house, is the most striking feature.

PULLIAM HOUSE     8
*217 S. 3rd Street*
*1856 (moved to 2701 E. Franklin Street)*

This house is a remnant of a fine residential street of the past. Bequeathed to the Association for the Preservation of Virginia Antiquities in 1938, it was later restored by the Universal Leaf Tobacco Company. The superb ornamental cast-iron, characteristic of the 1850's, is un-excelled in Richmond. A proposed expressway will cause demolition of this house. It may be rebuilt on Church Hill.

HENRY COALTER CABELL HOUSE       9
*116 S. 3rd Street*
*1847*

Some hint of the nineteenth-century residential grandeur of Gamble's Hill is suggested by this mansion. It was one of the first houses to be preserved in Richmond through being made over for offices by a business company. Architecturally it is different from anything else in the city, with its two-story wings and Egyptian columns. The balcony, bay windows, and large exten-sion in the back are later additions.

BOLLING HAXALL HOUSE       10
*211 E. Franklin Street*
*1858*

A mansion of the 1850's in the florid Victorian Italianate style, this house exemplifies the changing taste of the times, after years of building in the staid Greek Revival

manner. The small yard is enclosed by a fine cast-iron fence. Since 1900 the building has served as the Woman's Club.

108, 110, AND 112 E. CARY STREET          11
*c. 1870, 1859, and 1853*

These three mid-nineteenth-century houses have been remodeled and successfully adapted for modern office use. Together they compose into an effective street façade. The older ones, at 110 and 112, are in no sense restorations, having been altered from their original appearance.

## CROZET HOUSE (CURTIS CARTER HOUSE)  12
*100 E. Main Street*
*1814-15*

One of the best examples of its period surviving in Richmond, this house was restored in 1940 and is used for offices. The Flemish bond brickwork, window lintels, and interior woodwork are noteworthy features. The entrance treatment derives from earlier Georgian precedents and is not in character with the original design.

Here from 1828 to 1832 lived Claudius Crozet, noted French engineer who served the Commonwealth of Virginia.

## 8-12 N. SECOND STREET  13
*1848 (moved to 2608-10 E. Franklin and 2515 E. Grace)*

Originally this was a row of four houses with gable roof and dormers. One was demolished and two of the others have had the gable replaced by a full third story.

Although a restoration here would be a great asset to the city, present plans for the expansion of the Richmond City Library will result in the demolition of this group.

LINDEN ROW                                              14
*100-114 E. Franklin Street*
*1847 and 1853*

Extraordinary cityscape, an example of Greek Revival town-house grouping that is probably not surpassed anywhere in the United States. On completion, the row occupied the full block and consisted of ten similar dwellings, although built in two groups of five by different owners in different years. Two of the houses at the east end were razed in 1922 for construction of an office building, architecturally an unworthy successor.

The dwelling group is remarkable for its unity: rhythm of the white wood porticoes on granite base and steps, the whole tied together by the front planting area, iron fence, stone wall.

The row, minus two houses, has been kept intact by a preservation-minded owner, who has adapted the units for office and dwelling use without exterior alteration.

## 11, 13, AND 15 E. FRANKLIN STREET 15
*1840, 1847, and 1837*

Three renovated houses which date from before the middle of the 19th century, these have had various changes made in later years, including addition of the fine iron veranda on the corner house.

## KENT-VALENTINE HOUSE 16
*12 E. Franklin Street*
*1845; architect: Isaiah Rogers*

Although much altered from its original appearance, this mansion retains the spirit of a vanished period. The third story was an early addition. After Granville G. Valentine bought the house in 1904 he raised the one-story wings and added the monumental portico. This portico replaced an iron veranda of exceptional beauty, which may have been as early as the house itself. The railing of the veranda has been retained on the present terrace.

ALLEN DOUBLE HOUSE                                    17
*4-6 E. Main Street*
*1836*

The oldest Greek Revival double house now standing in
Richmond. An example of the sacred and profane in
preservation, the western half shown here retains its
original and handsome appearance but the store-front
addition on the other part is a desecration.

QUARLES HOUSE                                        18
*1 E. Main Street*
*1839 (demolished 1968)*

This is an early example of the Greek Revival style
which has had later alterations, apparently in the late

1850's. The main cornice and that of the porch, as well as the lengthened first-floor windows, seem to date from that time, and probably the attractive balcony railing also.

## ELLEN GLASGOW HOUSE 19
*1 W. Main Street*
*1841*

This well-preserved Greek Revival house, with Doric portico and hipped roof, was the home of novelist Ellen Glasgow. Restored and maintained by the William Byrd Branch of the Association for the Preservation of Virginia Antiquities, it is used ·as headquarters by the Richmond Area University Center. The carriage house and enclosed rear garden are notable features.

## 111 NORTH ADAMS STREET 20
*c. 1870 (demolished)*

This little building is notable because it is one of a diminishing number of carriage houses left standing in central Richmond. This one was accessory to a house on a corner lot, thus it had a prominent location and was given suitable embellishment: bracketed loft window, cornice, and pediment.

JEFFERSON HOTEL                                    21
*100 block of W. Franklin Street*
*1895*
*architects: Carrère and Hastings*

The Jefferson is one of Richmond's landmarks and a great period-piece. It was built by Major Lewis Ginter, tobacconist and philanthropist, who had risen from poverty to great wealth; he selected a renowned architectural firm to design the hotel and spared no expense to make it a civic asset to Richmond.

A design from the heyday of architectural eclecticism, it has both Spanish and Italian echoes. The lavish building was first opened in 1895; most of it was gutted by fire in 1901, then rebuilt. Many notables have stayed here, including it is said, five U.S. presidents.

MAYO MEMORIAL HOUSE                          22
*110 W. Franklin Street*
*1845*

Here is a variation of Greek Revival dwelling design:
the temple form with monumental portico. It was not
common in Richmond and this is the only example remaining. However, except for the portico, the appearance of this mansion has suffered badly from alterations
made in the eighties. Originally it had low flanking
wings; a story was added to these, bringing their roof
level up to that of the central portion. At the same time
the window openings were altered and the interior was
made over to accord with Victorian taste. It is now used
for church offices.

200 W. FRANKLIN STREET                       23
*c. 1875*

This solid Victorian townhouse completes an interesting
and varied block. The cast-iron fence and wrought-iron
gate are notable.

COLE DIGGS HOUSE                                    24
*204 W. Franklin Street*
*c. 1809*

This is one of the two oldest houses on Franklin Street. The two-story veranda in front was added in the mid-nineteenth century.

DANIEL CALL HOUSE                                  25
*217 W. Grace Street*
*before 1796*

The two-story front portion of this building is preserved from the eighteenth century and is one of a very few frame houses remaining in Richmond from that time. It was moved here from its original site at Ninth and Capitol Streets in 1849, and has served in several capacities: first as a dwelling, then successively as a church, private school, and funeral home. The entrance porch, rear wing, and one-story annex are all later additions.

PALMER HOUSE 26
*211 W. Franklin Street*
*1852*

This is an exceptionally well-preserved three-story town house in the Greek Revival style. The entrance portico is especially noteworthy.

LYONS HOUSE 27
*301 W. Franklin Street*
*1858 (demolished)*

This restored house is chiefly notable for its ornamental iron veranda. Produced mostly by local foundries, such ironwork was extensively used on Richmond houses from the late fifties into the eighties.

BALTIMORE ROW                                    28
*305-9 W. Franklin Street*
*c. 1875   (demolished)*

Here is a post-Civil War row house of a type unusual in
Richmond. The French mansard roof was popular in
America from the seventies through the nineties. The
marble steps are reminiscent of Baltimore.

COMMONWEALTH CLUB                                29
*401 W. Franklin Street*
*1890*

An interesting and vigorous period piece, this building
has both Italian Renaissance and Romanesque motifs.
The west wing is a recent addition of sensitive design:
it is contemporary in character, while harmonizing with
the older building.

400 W. FRANKLIN STREET                    30
*c. 1870 (demolished)*

With its stucco front, scroll-saw veranda, and framed
windows with rounded heads, this Victorian house has
considerable charm.

# West Along the James

## Oregon Hill

Oregon Hill, a bluff with a magnificent view of the James, is at the north end of the Robert E. Lee Bridge. Separated from Gamble's Hill to the east by a ravine, it was further isolated from the city when the state penitentiary was built across its north slope in the last years of the eighteenth century.

Because of these barriers, development of the hill was slow in coming. It did come, and with a sudden rush

*Virginia Penitentiary*

commencing in 1838, when a housing boom here followed the construction of the Tredegar Iron Works at the foot of the hill between the canal and the river. The industry chose this site in order to use the water power of the river falls. In its day it was one of Richmond's foremost industries; it was vital to Confederate armament production, and it employed over a thousand workers as late as the 1890's.

Though not a company enterprise, the settlement that mushroomed on the heights above the factory was mostly populated by Tredegar workers and their families. Today can be seen the remnant of this village within a city, along Maiden Lane, Church and First Streets, with a few houses still standing on Belvidere. Practically all of these were built between 1838 and 1850, and together.they make a museum of workers' dwellings of that period.

Over the past century the changes that have come to Oregon Hill have been of two kinds. One was sudden and drastic: the entire southern half of the neighborhood was cleared away in the early 1950's to prepare the site of the Virginia War Memorial. The other change has been a gradual one of neglect and deterioration, to be seen all too clearly in what is left. There remains a picturesque massing of buildings on a splendid site.

VIRGINIA WAR MEMORIAL
*Belvidere Street, north of Robert E. Lee Bridge*
*1955*
*architect: S. J. Collins*

Built by the State of Virginia to commemorate the Virginians who lost their lives in World War II and Korea, this memorial contains mementoes from the principal battle areas and American military cemeteries throughout the world and a monumental statue, "Memory," created by the sculptor Leo Friedlander. The Memorial occupies a magnificent site, providing a panoramic view of the James River.

Sydney

The neighborhood known as Sydney lies between Hollywood Cemetery and Belvidere Street. The latter separ-
ates it from Oregon Hill. Sometime after Colonel William Byrd II founded Richmond, his son built his home,
which he called "Belvidere," here near the present intersection of Belvidere and China Streets. The house
burned in 1854, but long before this a subsequent owner
had commenced the subdivision of its lands: the name
Sydney was given to the first such subdivision, which was
made in 1817.

There was not extensive development, however, until close to mid-century. Like Orgeon Hill, Sydney was
built up with the modest homes of workmen. Today the
interior streets hold much of their nineteenth-century
character.

SPRING STREET HOME
*601 Spring Street*
*1818*

This house, the oldest now standing in the Sydney
neighborhood, was built by Samuel Parsons, who was
superintendent of the penitentiary nearby. It has been
altered, but the two entrances, at the front and side,
probably date from the original construction.

## 417 S. PINE STREET
*1856*

This quaint Gothic cottage is a rather singular survival. The modern covering obscures the board and batten walls which gave it much of its character.

## HOLLYWOOD CEMETERY
*1854*

This beautiful tract overlooking the James has more the look of a park than a burial ground. It was laid out by an eminent Philadelphia architect, John Notman, who was retained to redesign Capitol Square at about the same time. Notman's design was undoubtedly influenced by the landscape architect Andrew Jackson Downing. Notman also designed a romantic Gothic "ruin" to embellish the gateway; its remains are embedded in the building beside the former entrance at the end of Spring Street.

Many notable persons are buried here: Jefferson Davis, Presidents James Monroe and John Tyler, Commodore Matthew Fontaine Maury, and General J. E. B.

Stuart. Eighteen thousand Confederate dead lie in Hollywood, their resting place marked by an impressive pyramid of rough granite blocks.

President Monroe died in 1831 and was buried in New York. His body was brought to his native state in 1858 and reinterred in this cemetery with appropriate ceremony. The grave is marked by an unusual, and handsome, monument of cast iron. It was designed by Richmond architect Albert Lybrock.

# Monroe Park West

## Monroe Park

At the time of the Civil War a large public space known as Monroe Square extended south from Broad Street at the western edge of the city. For several years before the war this served as a fairgrounds. It was used as a military encampment during the war years. Shortly afterward, Belvidere, Franklin, and Laurel Streets were extended, shaping the five-sided space that is now called Monroe Park.

Today Monroe Park is a rather ambivalent city space. It serves to some extent as a neighborhood park and part time as a college campus; for the rest it can be described as an open space with trees in it. Its architectural frame is chaotic on two sides, east and south. It serves as the spacious forecourt for two buildings of

*Fairgrounds in 1854, now Monroe Park*

distinctive character, the Mosque and Sacred Heart Cathedral. It is the beginning of the Fan District, the "palm of the hand" from which this unique residential section fans out to the west.

Richmond Professional Institute, centered a block west on Franklin Street, has been growing toward the park. For many years a small school housed in old residences, this state-owned college is now faced with enormous growth demands, reflected in the new dormitory at the Laurel-Franklin corner of the park. The development of RPI, its future direction, shape, and form will be the most significant influence on the future character of Monroe Park and the lower Fan District.

THE MOSQUE
*Laurel Street at W. Main Street*
*1928*
*architect: Marcellus Wright, Sr.*

Notable as an architectural curio, this building reflects the rampant eclecticism of the 1920's. It was designed as a Shrine Temple; hence the Near Eastern decor. It now serves the city as an auditorium and office building.

SACRED HEART CATHEDRAL
*Laurel Street at Floyd and Park*
*1903*

In 1905 this replaced St. Peter's, which still stands at
Grace and Eighth, as the Cathedral of the Richmond
Diocese of the Roman Catholic Church. It is a Richmond landmark, with its impressive dome and visible
site.

The Fan District

The neighborhood that Richmond people call "the Fan"
extends west from Monroe Park to Boulevard. Its name
derives from the street configuration with Main diverging
from Franklin and Monument Avenue to form its edges.

An annexation in 1867 brought this area into the city
as far west as Lombardy. Subsequent annexations were
made in 1892 and 1906 as development continued west

to Boulevard and beyond. Intensive building in the Fan District did not begin until the 1880's; the western end was ultimately built up in the 1920's. After World War II, Richmond's suburbs had sprawled so far from the center that some residents began to look for dwellings closer in. The pleasant tree-lined streets and the commodious town houses in the Fan proved attractive; in the past two decades it has become fashionable as well as convenient, with the result that numerous older houses have been repaired and modernized.

Some of the late nineteenth-century houses are interesting, especially those with ornamental iron or scroll-saw wood verandas. The later rows may tend toward monotony; they are certainly not outstanding as architecture. However, the Fan owes its special character not so much to the individual buildings as to some less easily defined quality of cityscape, a quiet harmony and appropriateness of the whole. This comes, in some measure, from the layout of the streets. It is fortuitous and accidental rather than from considered design. The direction changes in Grove and Floyd and terminations of

several cross streets at Park produce closures and vistas that intrigue the eye. Park Avenue, laid out along an earlier country road, inherits a sequence of gentle turns which makes travel along it a delightful experience.

## WEST FRANKLIN STREET
*Monroe Park to Stuart Circle*

The segment of Franklin Street just west of Monroe Park has exceptional character in the way that its architectural pieces, though showing variety and individuality, are unified by a harmony of scale and materials. This quality is being vitiated by the rebuilding operations of Richmond Professional Institute. The turn of events is ironical, because the school has been in past years a real factor in preservation through its adaptation of existing buildings for classrooms and dormitories.

Before the tearing down and building to a larger scale set in, the architecture of these four blocks was almost wholly an heritage of the 1890-1910 period. An exception is the Ritter-Hickock house, a mansion built when this was still a rural area.

## RITTER-HICKOCK HOUSE
*821 W. Franklin Street*
*1855*

Built as a suburban mansion, this is now part of the Richmond Professional Institute.

## LEWIS GINTER HOUSE
*901 W. Franklin Street*
*c. 1890*

This solid and imposing mansion of brick and brownstone is probably the best one surviving from its period. It was the home of Major Lewis Ginter, who made his fortune in the tobacco business and built the Jefferson Hotel. It is now part of the Richmond Professional Institute.

## BETH AHABAH SYNAGOGUE
*W. Franklin at Ryland Street*
*1904*

Much monumental religious building was done in Richmond during the early decades of the twentieth century. This neoclassic synagogue is well situated, making a visual focus at the end of Ryland Street.

BROAD STREET STATION
*W. Broad Street at Davis Avenue*
*1917-19*
*architect: John Russell Pope*

Richmond's second monumental railroad terminal is a
Roman adaptation, designed by a well-known eclectic
monumentalist.

MONUMENT AVENUE

Starting as an extension of Franklin Street, Monument
Avenue was named when the Lee Monument was placed
at the Allen Avenue intersection in 1890. Over the next
forty years four other monuments honoring Confederate
figures were placed along this spacious boulevard. It is
unquestionably one of America's most splendid streets,
deriving its distinction not so much from its architecture, which is mostly undistinguished, as from its
breadth, landscaping, and thematic rhythm of monuments. The sculpture of the individual memorials varies
in quality.

J. E. B. STUART
*Lombardy Street*
*1907*
*sculptor: Fred Moynihan*

ROBERT E. LEE
*Allen Avenue*
*1890*
*sculptor: Jean Antoine Mercie*

JEFFERSON DAVIS
*Davis Street*
*1907*
*sculptor: Edward V. Valentine*

STONEWALL JACKSON
*Boulevard*
*1919*
*sculptor: Frederick Wm. Sievers*

MATTHEW FONTAINE MAURY
*Belmont Avenue*
*1929*
*sculptor: Frederick Wm. Sievers*

COLUMBIA
*W. Grace Street at Lombardy*
*1817*

This was one of the finer residences of its time in Richmond, both in its exterior appearance and interior woodwork. In 1834 it was acquired for a seminary, which became Richmond College in 1840 and later the University of Richmond. The University was located here until it moved to its suburban site in 1914. It still owns and makes use of this building. The mansion has served many uses: classrooms, later a professor's residence, a hospital during the Civil War, and barracks for Union troops in 1865.

It is almost the only survival of historic importance west of the Capitol on Grace Street, one of Richmond's finest streets before World War I.

The house has suffered some changes with the removal of chimneys and a captain's walk with balustrade. The entrance, originally on Lombardy Street, has been changed to the Grace Street side.

TALAVERA
*2315 W. Grace Street*
*1838*

This house has a more definite connection with Edgar Allan Poe than any other now standing in the city. He was a friend of Susan Archer Talley and was a frequent visitor here in 1849.

This was a farm house, which urban growth has now surrounded. Its appearance has been mutilated by changes: entrance terrace, balustrade, window sash, and decoration on the roof ridges. The original beaded wood siding has been covered, or replaced, by asbestos shingles.

## THREE TOWN HOUSES
*2309, 2315 and 2601 Monument Avenue*
*1917, 1923 and 1924*
*William L. Bottomley*

These urbane mansions are representative of an architect who, supported by a wealthy clientele, was noted
for his impeccably styled domestic work, derived from
the Georgian or other historic models.

2309

2315

*2601 Monument Ave.*

## 2226 W. MAIN STREET
*1859*

Although board and batten houses were common in the latter half of the nineteenth century, few of them remain. This one is well-preserved.

CONFEDERATE MEMORIAL CHAPEL
*Grove Avenue near Boulevard*
*1887*

Soldiers' Home was established in the 1880's for Confederate veterans on the site where the Virginia Museum now stands and continued there until the last inmate died in 1941. This little chapel was constructed with funds subscribed by veterans of the Confederate Army. Over the years funeral services for some 1700 veterans were held here. The chapel was restored and reopened in 1961. Some of the memorial stained-glass windows are contemporary with the building.

2905 AND 2911 GROVE AVENUE
*c. 1895*

These twin creations, in a once fashionable style known

as Queen Anne, seem today like stage sets for some fairy-tale play. Both houses are complemented by elaborate carriage houses in the rear.

# Chapter III

# Historic Preservation

## The Value of the Past

The time scale of Rome goes back over two milleniums, and the Eternal City owes its extraordinary richness to that fact. Or, more precisely, this richness is there because the architectural evidence, the tangible scenery, of this long history is there, and of course the history itself has been a particularly vivid one.

Age, like most things, is relative: a city founded two hundred years ago is considered new in Europe, but it is old in the context of America. And in this context, Richmond, established in colonial times, is an old city. Furthermore the historic importance of Richmond is great, both to the nation and to the state; the city has a preeminent place in the story of the nation's beginning and in the epic of the Civil War.

The buildings of the past may have value in terms of their historic associations or in terms of the quality of the architecture itself. Some in Richmond have both attributes; the Capitol, the John Marshall house, Masons' Hall, and the White House of the Confederacy are examples. The White House and Monumental Church as well have the further distinction of being representative works of a famous architect. Richmond is the poorer for having lost all of the buildings designed by the most distinguished of the nation's early architects, Benjamin Latrobe.

Some buildings, such as the Maury house, may have historic importance without having special quality in their architecture. St. John's Church is a special case: it is revered first of all for its place in an act of history, and secondly because it is probably the oldest building in Richmond. Its beauty is appealing and appropriate, and serves to make the site memorable, but this enhancement came at a later date.

There are many more buildings which are valuable as part of a varied architectural heritage but whose history is only of minor or local significance. Two eighteenth-century survivals in this category are the Old Stone House and the Craig house, both in the early town site in Shockoe Valley. These are simply vernacular representatives of domestic building of their era. But, in the Richmond time scale, their era was very early, and these are the only two left. And, being different from each other, each is unique. Each makes its own special contribution to the city.

The venerable age of the Craig house and the Old Stone House probably causes their value to be rather widely appreciated. They are symbols of the city's long past and ties to its village beginnings. What is not so generally recognized is that the city has a wealth of nineteenth-century buildings (though a diminishing wealth) that have value of a similar kind—as touch-stones with a particular segment of the past. In many cases these buildings are especially fine as architectural expressions of their segment of time, or they may simply be representative buildings which have become unique in the city through the destruction over time of others comparable.

Few cities in America today can boast Greek Revival domestic architecture as fine as the Barret house or Linden Row. The Hancock-Caskie house and the Ad-dolph Dill house, from different periods, are each unique survivals of design styles. The Bolling Haxall house represents the florid taste of its period, while Morson Row, built in the same decade, is the only row house of its style in the city, and a handsome building as well. The two Putney houses, part of the Medical College, are good Victorian town houses that have superb ornamental iron-work with meaning both in time and place, for this is the artistry of a Richmond industrial craft. Four churches in downtown Richmond from the two middle decades of the century show four distinct architectural styles—First Baptist, Second Presbyterian, St. Paul's, and Broad Street Methodist—each one is a notable example, and each one contributes to Richmond a measure of individuality and identity. A few iron-front buildings on Main Street are the heritage of a brief period and transient character of American commercial building; some need restoration, parts have been badly remodeled, while some have been handsomely treated by the present-day tenants. But all of them, and not so many remain, evoke a particular past that is a part of Richmond.

This is not an exhaustive listing; it could be extended considerably. The buildings just mentioned, and many others, are the visible evidence of the city's history and past life; they mark and emphasize the city's time dimension. Their presence enriches the city; the loss of any one of them makes it a poorer place.

Finally, there is the simple matter of good appearance. Much has been said and written about the chaotic ugliness of the modern American city. It is true, at least of parts, of all cities. The full impact of this visual horror usually comes along highways that have developed as commercial strips. Richmond has, in Broad Street, an avenue that can compete with the worst anywhere.

If in this book there is a concentration on the urban scenery that survives from Richmond's past, chiefly before the twentieth century, the reason lies in the fact that this architectural heritage is both rich and pleasant. The speed and haste of the contemporary era and its technology have been rubbing out this scenery at an alarming rate. They have produced many things that would have been the envy of our ancestors but, at the same time, have failed to build an environment which can compare in terms of beauty. Perhaps more important, the forces of the twentieth-century way of life have tended to produce a universal sameness. All modern cities, insofar as they serve as habitats for automobiles, tend to look alike. If our older cities, Richmond among them, are to retain unique character and individuality, they would do well to look to the preservation of their architectural heritage of the past, or whatever residue may still remain.

## Historic Preservation in Richmond

The year 1889 marks the beginning of historic preservation in Richmond. In that year the city government
considered tearing down the White House of the Confederacy. The city had acquired the mansion in 1861
and had leased it to the Confederate government. At
the end of the war it was seized by the Federal government; by 1871 it had been returned to the city and put
into use as a public school. In time the building needed
repair and fireproofing; the school board wanted to
demolish it and put up a new building on the site. Fortunately the wisdom of a city council majority prevailed
and the historic mansion was eventually given to the Confederate Memorial Literary Society for use as a museum.
After restoration the Confederate Museum was opened
there in 1896.

In the meantime two other historic residences had
been preserved for posterity through the generous actions
of their owners. Mann S. Valentine II died in 1892,
leaving his residence, with an endowment, to serve as
a museum to house his various collections. Thus began
the Valentine Museum, and thus was preserved the Wickham house, which, like the White House of the Confederacy, is a priceless symbol of Richmond's history and
an architectural specimen of great quality from the
Federal era. The following year another historic house in
downtown Richmond was given by its owner, Mrs.
John Stewart, to the Virginia Historical Society. This
is the house where General Lee lived briefly following the
Civil War.

The next episode in local preservation came in 1907,
when the John Marshall house was threatened with
destruction. Once again the need for a school site was
the cause of the threat; this time the city purchased the
house in the course of assembling land for a new high
school. The high school, named for John Marshall, was
eventually built on the northern half of the block, but
opposition to the demolition of the house led the city
to turn it over to the Association for the Preservation of
Virginia Antiquities in 1911. That organization restored

it and maintains it today as a historic shrine.

The saving of the John Marshall house marks the first local endeavor of the APVA. The association was the first state preservation society in the South; its founding in 1889 had been motivated by the need to protect the remains of the Virginia colonial settlement at Jamestown from the gradual erosion of the river bank.

The circumstances of the near destruction of the John Marshall house should give us pause for reflection today. In 1907 the need for the high school was urgent, whereas the old house, the eighteenth-century home of Chief Justice Marshall, was considered by many to be of no important value to Richmond. Less than sixty years later the school building has been dismantled, no longer needed in this area, and there are .plans for restoring and landscaping the now vacant land, giving back to the house the garden and outbuildings it had in the long ago past.

The second house to be saved by the APVA is Richmond's oldest dwelling, the Old Stone House, at 1916 E. Main Street. It was bought at auction in 1911 and rented for a number of years as an antique shop. Since 1921 it has been the headquarters of the Poe Foundation and a library and museum of Edgar Allan Poe memorabilia.

The Association for the Preservation of Virginia Antiquities is a state-wide organization; much of its work is done through its local chapters. The Richmond chapter, called the William Byrd Branch, was formed in 1935, and it has since been the major influence in historic preservation locally. The branch was born of another imminent demolition crisis. The Craig house, built around 1785 and unique in Richmond, had deteriorated almost to the point of collapse. The William Byrd Branch bought the house and restored it along with its garden and outbuilding. In the years since, the branch has acquired and restored three additional houses and has secured tenants for them. The Ann Carrington house on Church Hill and the Ellen Glasgow house were purchased in 1943 and 1947 respectively, each by means of a subscription campaign. The Pulliam house had earlier been given the APVA by its owner; in 1953 it was

turned over to the branch for restoration and mainten-
ance.

The William Byrd Branch APVA does not consider
its chief purpose to be the accumulation of property.
Its aim is to stimulate the interest of the public—individuals and organizations—so that they will buy, restore, and utilize the worthwhile old buildings of Richmond. This aim has been realized in the saving of a
considerable number of fine buildings in the heart of
Richmond and putting them to use for business purposes. Thus individuals have bought and preserved the
Barret and Clarke houses on Fifth between Cary and
Main, Linden Row on Franklin Street, the Crozet house
at First and Main, and houses at 13 and 15 E. Franklin.
Although the William Byrd Branch was not directly in-
volved in the purchase and restoration of these houses,
certainly its influence has played an important role.

Historic Richmond Foundation was created in 1956
for the specific purpose of reviving Church Hill as a good
residential neighborhood and stimulating restoration of
the houses there. The William Byrd Branch APVA had
previously bought and restored the Ann Carrington house
there. However, the methods of the APVA did not lend
themselves to the kind of extensive purchase and rehabilitation that was needed on Church Hill. Title to
all houses bought and restored by a branch must be
held by the parent APVA. Historic Richmond Foundation was formed as a nonprofit organization which can
act quickly to buy and sell property, thus getting reuse of
its capital, while placing the houses in the hands of
responsible owners who can restore them for their own
use. It simply spreads the base of the preservation program, making it operative for an entire neighborhood
rather than exclusively for a few individual buildings.

An early acquisition of Historic Richmond Foundation was the Hilary Baker house, next to the Ann Carrington house and contemporary with it. This house had
been extensively altered; title was made over to the
APVA, whose William Byrd Branch restored it to its
original appearance in 1959. By the beginning of 1967
Historic Richmond Foundation had through purchase

preserved twelve houses on Church Hill, and individual members and friends had acquired others. The restorations have worked wonders in appearance, the trend toward deterioration of the neighborhood has been checked and reversed, and a revived Church Hill is showing signs of becoming a prestige neighborhood.

In 1957 the combined efforts of the APVA and Historic Richmond Foundation brought the passage by City Council of an ordinance designating the St. John's Church District for special protection under historic zoning. The ordinance established a Commission of Architectural Review; within the designated area, which embraces most of Church Hill, all requests for building construction, demolition, and exterior alteration must be considered by this commission.

## Problems of Preservation

Some of the most notable buildings yield full continuity with the past in that they still continue to serve their original function. Examples are the Capitol, the Governor's Mansion, Masons' Hall, and some, but not all, of the historic churches. Obviously preservation in itself is not a problem here. There are two problems, however, which do arise from time to time. One of these is technological—that of mechanical modernization. The other concerns the appropriateness of design when additions are needed to meet demands for increased space. Both the Capitol and St. Paul's Church have had sizable additions to the original buildings. The St. Paul's church school and office addition, forming with the older church a garden court, is exceptionally well-handled. Another successful example of adding to an older building may be seen at the Commonwealth Club on W. Franklin Street; here an effective addition has been made in a design that is harmonious with the original while being fully contemporary in spirit.

A few buildings, when continuation of their former use is not practicable, may be restored and preserved as shrines or museums. The John Marshall and the Wickham houses and the White House of the Confederacy have survived by this means. Situated as they are in the heart of the city these mansions could hardly have continued as residences. Making them museums has not only assured their preservation but has at the same time added a cultural dimension to Richmond by making them accessible to the public. Obviously this kind of sanctification is limited to only a few historic buildings in the city.

The way a city grows, or whether or not it grows, has in our American tradition always had much to do with how much, and what, of its older architecture is allowed to remain standing. Colonial Williamsburg, as a museum city, Virginia showpiece, and national tourist attraction, might not exist had not the seat of Virginia's government been moved to Richmond just after the new nation came into being. Williamsburg slumbered as a peaceful small town for a hundred and fifty years until the Rockefeller restoration went into operation. The restoration architects found there a considerable architectural heritage left intact from the eighteenth century.

By contrast Richmond's growth from town to metropolis has been accompanied by the obliteration and rebuilding of much of its older areas. This process has occurred most completely where commerce or industry has overrun neighborhoods of dwellings. Church Hill has largely escaped this fate. Until recently this reprieve has been the result of fortuitous circumstance. Effective planning and zoning were unknown before World War II, and the zoning map today condones and supports the inappropriate intrusions which had earlier come in along Marshall and Broad Streets in the St. John's Church area. Otherwise Church Hill has remained from its beginning almost solidly residential in character. Thus its surviving heritage of architecture is relatively large. Church Hill suffered in the early twentieth century from neglect and deterioration rather than destruction from a change in use. Through positive preservation measures this decline was arrested in the 1950's. Since then there has been much progress toward revival: Carrington Square, the pilot restoration block, has been nearly completed; the 2300 Club and the Hand Work Shop enterprises represent desirable activities as well as restorations; numerous other houses on the hill along Grace and Franklin Streets have been purchased and quite a few of them restored. Certain built-in characteristics enhance the prospect on Church Hill for continued upgrading, as well as enlargement of the area affected. A location convenient to the center of the city, topographic insulation from industry and commerce, the quiet amenity of many of the streets, the domestic scale and pleasure of the urban scenery that derive from the old buildings: all of these are strong and positive factors which support revival efforts. Important also are the precedents in other cities, notably the success stories of Georgetown and Beacon Hill. The essential ingredients for fulfillment of the Church Hill program are adequate private funds and effective public action through planning and zoning.

There are other sections of central Richmond which share with Church Hill this residential continuity with the past. The Fan District is comparable except that its past is a more recent one. It does possess similar amenities, and its preservation and future improvement seem to rest on similar efforts. However, the expansion of the Richmond Professional Institute will have particular impact on the eastern portion in the vicinity of Monroe Park. An increase to several times the present enrollment, reaching 35,000 by 1985, is anticipated. Until about 1960 this institution was accommodated almost wholly in older residential buildings, thus fitting in well with the texture of the existing neighborhood. But recent construction has been of an altogether different character and scale.

There are two situations where valuable buildings in the historic heritage are especially vulnerable to the forces of change. Here the preservation problems are both difficult and urgent. The first case is the preservation of residential survivals in areas where the basic character of the neighborhood itself has changed, where commercial transition has intruded, or where increase in land values has led to apartment construction. The second case is that of old commercial buildings, which, though they may be important as architecture and as cityscape, are frequently obsolescent in terms of the economics of real estate.

In Richmond the area from Capitol Square to Belvidere Street, from Grace Street south to the river, has undergone such extensive transformation that only random pieces of the earlier city remain. Zoning as a protective device is no longer applicable, except perhaps for a few blocks on Franklin Street; these blocks are still residential, but the lid has already been lifted from bulk and height controls, so that new apartment buildings have been replacing the older town houses. Elsewhere adaptive use seems the only possible defense. The precedent for this is considerable; Linden Row, the Bolling Haxall, Hancock-Caskie, Barret, and Scott houses, and numerous others have been preserved by this means.

Only a few scattered remnants of commercial buildings of pre-Civil War Richmond are still standing. Fire and obsolescence together have disposed of the rest of them. And it is obsolescence which today threatens the blocks of Main and Cary Streets where there remain store, office, and warehouse structures erected during the decade or so following the Civil War. Since much of this area has been relatively stagnant the threat has come only in recent years, and as yet there has been no organized effort directed toward preserving these buildings. There are many buildings which deserve such an effort; these are mostly on Main Street from Ninth east to Shockoe Valley and on Cary in the blocks east of Tenth Street. Adaptive use here is, once again, a preservation hope. This has successfully occurred in a number of the iron-front buildings on Main Street, and it has resulted in several offices of distinction. Especially notable results have been achieved at 911, 1007, 1015, and 1311 E. Main.

These adaptations have been carefully and tastefully done. There are, however, many more occupants who, although they have put the buildings to productive use, have so altered the fronts at street level that the original fine character has been destroyed.

In the long run if any part of the century-old com-

mercial architecture in central Richmond is to be preserved it is clear that new and imaginative measures
must be found. Zoning, in its traditional and hackneyed
application, is useless in this situation. A more positive
approach would be a precise control over the location
of parking lots and garages, confining them to certain
blocks on specific streets. Richmond would also profit
by giving attention to what is happening in other cities.
Savannah provides an example of successful use, by individual and private entrepreneurs, of old commercial
buildings. In that city fine restaurants are operating in
warehouse districts; here perhaps is the salvation of
the Shockoe Slip area. Finally, some unity of purpose
must be expressed through an organization formed for
the sole purpose of directing and co-ordinating a preservation program for this section of the city. The
Church Hill revival did not effectively materialize until
the Historic Richmond Foundation was organized.

## Public Institutions as Destroyers and Preservers

In many cases the conservation of good cityscape elements and of individual buildings depends directly on
government or public institutions. The Richmond Professional Institute, as a state institution, is a case in point.
Similarly the Medical College of Virginia, which has
preserved its Egyptian Building and Monumental Church,
owns other landmarks whose tenure may be less secure:
Thomas U. Walter's old First Baptist Church, the two
fine Putney houses, the former Sheltering Arms Hospital,
and the picturesque Howitzers Armory. The City of
Richmond will build a new city hall; there is the necessity
of adapting the present one for continued office use and
also of finding for the city-owned Broad Street Methodist
Church an adequate contemporary use. Both of these
landmarks would have been demolished had an earlier
scheme for the civic center gone ahead. The city's
coliseum will fill two blocks and replace old buildings;
in this case the site had already become a mishmash of
mixed uses and deterioration. The construction of the

coliseum will undoubtedly accelerate rebuilding and change in the surrounding blocks.

An instance where the city government itself will make a direct decision on preservation is the case of the row house group at 8—12 N. Second Street. These little townhouses stand on land intended for expansion of the main library. They could be restored and would be a handsome asset to the city. Imaginative planning and creative urban design could incorporate them into the library group and make them useful as well as attractive. However, present plans seem to indicate that they will be demolished.

The decade of the sixties is witnessing an extensive growth of the state's administrative office facilities, expressed in a formal and grandiose disposition of tall new buildings, fanning out to the east of Capitol Square. This plan originally called for a huge acreage of surface parking space which would have eliminated both Morson Row and City Hall. A revised plan issued in 1966 suffers these landmarks to remain and sensibly places the parking in multi-story buildings which do not face on the square itself.

Finally, the state's Department of Highways has the final authority for locating expressways within the city. In Richmond, as elsewhere, these networks bring a vast disruption to the existing fabric of the city. As this book goes to press a route for the western expressway access into downtown Richmond has been chosen by the highway engineers. This route cuts a block-wide swathe between Canal and Byrd Streets and Belvidere to Shockoe Valley. Lying in its destructive path are several historic structures, including the Pulliam house and the last remains of the canal system. These canal locks should be recognized and preserved as something of special historical value to the city. The Planning Commission with the help of consultants has proposed a plan for park development which would include restoration of these fine granite canal locks; a rather slight adjustment in the highway alignment would permit this. But the City of Richmond is suffering from severe civic schizophrenia in regard to its James River waterfront.

It could be developed as a spacious recreation asset. Yet it remains almost wholly inaccessible to public use—a dirty, unsightly, unplanned and festering wasteland. There is a crying need for some kind of plan which will weigh and balance the conflict of uses and pressures and possibilities. The waterfront should be put to its highest and best use.

## *Historic Preservation in Richmond, 1976*

Present-day visitors to Richmond are always impressed by the wealth of historic buildings in the city's downtown neighborhoods and business districts, a fact that amazes many natives who have watched so many important structures come down in recent years. But despite regrettable losses, many corners of the central business district yet retain a traditional flavor, and Capitol Square, the focal point of the area, with its Jeffersonian centerpiece and frame of architectural monuments, can be matched by few other cities.

A number of key buildings are by no means secure, however. The future of the very symbol of Richmond's recovery from Reconstruction, the exuberant Old City Hall with its handsome interiors, remains in doubt, and the nearby Old First Baptist Church, designed by the nationally prominent Thomas U. Walter, occupies the site of a proposed building for the Medical College of Virginia. In marked contrast, however, Robert Mills's famed Monumental Church is being restored for expanded use by the college.

As this book went to press in 1968 Professor Dulaney was especially concerned with the demolition taking place in the path of the Downtown Expressway below Main Street and in the area around the Richmond Coliseum site north of Broad Street. The expressway, now virtually complete, caused the loss of several entries in this guide, the most important of which were three stone locks and two turning basins of the historic James

River and Kanawha Canal. The commendable efforts of the Reynolds Metals Company in restoring a section of this canal system adjacent to their North Plant along Byrd Street failed to convince expressway officials that a completely restored and operating canal could be a major attraction for the city. Significant as was this loss, Reynolds's project has been immensely beneficial for showing how a corporate giant can also be a good neighbor. Another illustration is the Ethyl Corporation's restoration of the New Gun Foundry and other sections of the Tredegar Iron Works, a complex of Civil War–era industrial buildings at the foot of their headquarters on Gamble's Hill.

Considering that the development of the Main Street to the James River area has meant the clearance of most existing structures there, the survival of the Shockoe Slip district centering on Thirteenth and E. Cary Streets is all the more remarkable. Private initiative in this colorful area has been instrumental in the renovation of the district's brick stores and warehouses into attractive restaurants and shops. Similar activity is taking place in the adjacent financial district on Main Street. There the restoration of the richly decorated Stearns Block for luxury offices is a demonstration that Richmond's noted iron-ornamented buildings can be adapted to compete with their more modern neighbors.

The construction of Richmond's new Coliseum, itself a notably handsome work of architecture, has failed to stimulate expected building activity in the surrounding area. This is a particularly lamentable situation because many fine old dwellings were pulled down to clear the path for development; only dusty parking lots now form the Coliseum's setting. The location of the Coliseum in this area has, in any case, posed a threat to the stability of the Jackson Ward Historic District immediately to the west. Recent initiative to preserve this picturesque nineteenth-century neighborhood, unique in black history, came as an outgrowth of efforts to save the Maggie L. Walker House at 110 E. Leigh Street. Enthusiasm for the preservation of the home of this pioneer black business woman led to the formation of the Maggie L.

Walker Historical Association, a group that has since become an active preservation force for the entire Jackson Ward area.

The future of another landmark in the Coliseum area is not as promising. The Richmond Howitzers Armory, a fanciful castellated structure, is slated for demolition by a community college. Apparently little thought has been given to the adaptive use of this spacious and potentially useful building. In marked contrast, the comparable Blues Armory, just south of the Coliseum, is to be preserved and renovated.

The increasing interest in historic preservation shown by Richmond's citizens over the past several years has resulted in the city government's taking a more active role in this field. The city's hiring of an architectural historian to serve in the planning office and to act as secretary to the Commission of Architectural Review has brought much-needed expertise to the community. Citizens' rallying to prevent the distinctive paving blocks of Monument Avenue from being asphalted several years ago led the city to establish the Monument Avenue Commission, an advisory body concerned with the aesthetics of the entire avenue. On the negative side, the city chose to ignore the pleas of architects and historians and demolished the visually prominent Broad Street Methodist Church for a parking lot. The city in its expansion of the main library turned an indifferent eye toward the quaint row houses at 8-12 N. Second Street and forced them to be dismantled and moved to quarters on Church Hill. Fortunately, an increasingly enlightened attitude on the part of the city has put a restraint on such heavy-handed acts in recent years.

Paralleling this change of attitude within the city government is the increasingly sophisticated approach of private preservation groups. In 1974 the Historic Richmond Foundation hired its first full-time director and charged him with the responsibility not only of administering the foundation's long-term interests on Church Hill but of offering leadership in preservation activities throughout the city. The William Byrd Branch of the Association for the Preservation of Virginia Antiquities, perhaps the most energetic of the APVA's twenty-six branches, has taken its traditional goal of individual house restoration a step further by launching an ambitious project of preserving the group of early dwellings surrounding the branch's Adam Craig house. The rehabilitation of this important core of buildings is a key factor in the rebirth of the historic but deteriorating Shockoe Valley.

National attention has recently been focused on the conversion of abandoned railroad stations to new uses. The Commonwealth of Virginia is keeping in the forefront of this trend by proposing Broad Street Station to be the state's new science museum. The future of the equally notable yet equally abandoned Main Street Station is not so optimistic. As new elevated lanes of the Downtown Expressway curve irreverently near the clock tower, no plans for the building's future have been formulated. As with the Craig house, the successful adaptation of the station is crucial to the regeneration of Shockoe Valley.

But the expressway was not the only road project to threaten historic landmarks in recent years. In 1974 the John Woodward house, which only recently has been identified as the oldest frame house in the city, was spared demolition in the widening of Williamsburg Avenue by a gathering of preservation and civic groups. Fund-raising efforts are now in progress.

Franklin Street, from Linden Row to Belvidere, once Richmond's most fashionable address, has seen insensitive high-rise zoning shatter its historic ambience. One or two key blocks remain basically intact, however, and their preservation is the object of a concerted effort on behalf of several local groups including businessmen who see economic opportunity in the adaptive use of historic buildings. One especially happy note in Franklin Street's recent history has been the handsome restoration of the Kent-Valentine house by the Garden Club of Virginia as their state headquarters.

Richmond's extraordinary legacy has not gone unnoticed by the Commonwealth and the nation. In the last seven years sixty-one areas and individual buildings

in the city have been officially entered on the Virginia
Landmarks Register and the National Register of Historic Places.

Appendices

Index

# Description of the Surveys

An inventory of historic buildings in Richmond was initiated in 1964 and largely carried out in the spring of 1965. The work was jointly underwritten by the Association for the Preservation of Virginia Antiquities and its William Byrd Branch, Historic Richmond Foundation, and the Richmond City Planning Commission. Additional financial support came from the Old Dominion Foundation, specifically for publication of the results. The work was carried out under the direction of Paul S. Dulaney and Carlo Pelliccia of the School of Architecture, University of Virginia. Throughout the study T. Foster Witt, Chairman of the William Byrd Branch, APVA, coordinated liaison with the sponsoring organizations. The Valentine Museum furnished office space, and the Planning Commission provided maps and other valuable help.

Following an early surveillance of the entire city, the decision was made to confine the inventory to the central part of Richmond, from Boulevard east to Chimborazo Park, and from the James River north to Shockoe Cemetery. Richmond's historic architectural heritage is almost wholly contained within this area; furthermore, change and attrition have been occurring here with such rapidity that the need for documenting and evaluating the buildings and cityscape of the central city was obviously a matter for immediate attention.

The involvement of the Planning Commission as a sponsoring agency brought a widening of the horizon of the survey. The original concept was to document the individual buildings of historical and architectural interest. This documentation was carried through, but a parallel study was made at the same time of blocks, street frontages, and urban spaces in terms of aesthetic values. The objective of this second study was to record and analyze the assets which the city has in the way of appearance, and to do this in such a way that the record becomes a part of the basic planning survey and can be used in future city planning decisions. Ideally this should be followed by a design plan, part of the master plan of the city.

In the first survey, the inventory of historic buildings, about seven hundred and fifty items have been documented. The complete listing appears in Appendix B below. These include some objects of outdoor furnishing such as statuary and fountains as well as buildings. An invaluable source of information on the pre-Civil War architecture of Richmond has been the work of Miss Mary Wingfield Scott, including her books *Houses of Old Richmond* and *Old Richmond Neighborhoods* and a card file which she prepared with data on all of the buildings dating from before the Civil War. An effort to expand the record of buildings, significant either as architecture or for historic associations, up to the present time has been made, but it is not yet complete.

In the second survey, the one dealing with aesthetic resources, some thirty-six "survey units," or areas of central Richmond, were identified, analyzed, and documented with photographs, maps, and descriptions. Also, recommendations were made in regard to preservation and visual improvement.

Complete files of both compilations were prepared in duplicate, with copies placed in the custody of the Valentine Museum and the Richmond Planning Commission.

# Index to Survey of Historic Buildings

This is a listing of all buildings and items included in the inventory, showing street address and date of construction. The letter-numeral designation indicates the file number of each building and refers to the documentation which is maintained in the Valentine Museum. Buildings described in this volume appear in italic type.

A27     1003 Grove Ave.   1851

A28     Park Place Methodist Church, Monroe Park
        1887 (burned 1966)

A29     714 and 716 W. Franklin   c. 1895 (demolished)

A30     800 W. Franklin   c. 1890

A31     806 and 808 W. Franklin   c. 1890

A32     810 W. Franklin   c. 1900

*A33     Ritter-Hickock House, 821 W. Franklin St.   1855*

A34     828 W. Franklin   c. 1900

*A35     Ginter house, 901 W. Franklin   c. 1890*

A36     909 W. Franklin   c. 1900

A37     916 W. Franklin   c. 1900

A38     900 block of W. Franklin   c. 1900

A39     1000 W. Franklin   c. 1895

A40     1015 W. Franklin   c. 1910

A41     810, 812, and 814 W. Grace   late 19th cen.

*A42     Beth Ahabah Synagogue, 1201 W. Franklin   1904*

A43     St. James Episcopal Church, 1200 W. Franklin
        1912

A44     Memorial gate posts, 1100 block W. Grace

*A45     Columbia, W. Grace at Lombardy   1817*

*A46     Broad Street Station, W. Broad at Allen Ave.*
        *1917-19*

*A47     2226 W. Main   1859*

*A48     Talavera, 2315 W. Grace   1838*

A49     1935 Lake View Ave.   1848

B1      511 W. Marshall   c. 1855

B2      509 W. Marshall   1863

B3      505 W. Marshall   1865

B4      503 W. Marshall   1857

B5      501 W. Marshall   1856

B6      500 W. Marshall   1847

B7      405 to 413 W. Marshall   late 19th cen.

B8      403 W. Marshall   1855

B9      401 W. Marshall   1853

B10     414-16 W. Marshall   1856

B11     316 W. Marshall   1849

B12     315 to 21 W. Marshall   c. 1880

B13     313 W. Marshall   1817 and 1844(?)

B14     308-10 W. Marshall   1855

B15     306 W. Marshall   1848

B16    300-304 W. Marshall    1848
B17    320 W. Broad    1859
B18    409-11 and 413 N. Madison    1848-50
B19    216 W. Marshall    1849
B20    204 W. Marshall    1848
B21    Fire Station, 200 W. Marshall    late 19th cen.
B22    108 E. Clay    1848
B23    109 E. Clay    1848
B24    111-13 E. Clay    1848
B25    517 W. Clay    1856
B26    515 W. Clay    c. 1860
B27    513 W. Clay    1854
B28    509 W. Clay    1859
B29    505-7 W. Clay    1857
B30    503 W. Clay    1857
B31    419 W. Clay    1854
B32    307, 309, and 311 W. Clay    1845-46
B33    305 W. Clay    1846
B34    302 W. Clay    1842-43
B35    207-9 and 211-13 W. Clay    1839-41
B36    121 and 123 W. Clay    c. 1875
B37    107-11 W. Clay    c. 1875
B38    101 W. Clay    1859
B39    136-38 W. Clay    1820, altered c. 1855
*B40*    *106 to 114 W. Clay    late 19th cen.*
B41    509 N. Adams    1847
B42    Clay St. Methodist Church, W. Clay at Adams
       1859, altered 1890
*B43*    *14 W. Clay    1849*
*B44*    *12 W. Clay    1855*
*B45*    *8 and 10 W. Clay    1847*
*B46*    *15 and 21 W. Clay    1846-47*
B47    1 to 13 W. Clay    c. 1885
*B48*    *Addolph Dill house, 00 Clay    1832*
B49    7 E. Clay    1866
B50    553 Brook Ave.    1860
B51    408 W. Duval    1851
B52    319 W. Duval    1849
B53    133 W. Jackson    1813
*B54*    *Ebenezer Baptist Church, W. Leigh and Judah*
       *1873*

B55     227 W. Leigh    1846-47
B56     221 and 223 W. Leigh    1856
*B57     Armory, W. Leigh and St. Peter    1895*
B58     114 W. Leigh    1844
B59     521 Catherine    1860
B60     517 Catherine    1854
B61     515 Catherine    1854
B62     501 Catherine    1855
B63     500 Catherine    1845
B64     508-10 Catherine    1817-19
B65     516 Catherine    1819-21
B66     512 W. Leigh
B67     600 Brook Ave.    1841 and 1870
B68     407 to 413 W. Leigh    1848
B69     611 N. Henry    1847
B70     609 N. Henry    1847
B71     410 Catherine    1847
B72     516 N. Monroe    1846-47
B73     514 N. Monroe    late 19th cen.
B74     512 N. Monroe    1852
B75     515 and 517 N. Adams    1847
B76     Church, SW corner St. James and Leigh
B77     School, SW corner First and E. Leigh    late 19th cen.
B78     4 W. Leigh    1856
B79     5-7 W. Jackson    1859
B80     21 W. Jackson    1857
B81     613 Price    1860
B82     101½ W. Jackson    1835
B83     103 W. Jackson    c. 1865
B84     105 W. Jackson    1840
B85     104 W. Jackson    1840
B86     102 W. Jackson    1840
B87     704 N. Price    1860
B88     123 W. Duval    1846
B89     121 W. Duval    c. 1855
B90     111 W. Duval    1845
B91     109 W. Duval    1846
B92     107 W. Duval    1846
B93     Church, Duval at Cameo
B94     26 W. Jackson    1849

B95    20 and 22 W. Jackson    1848
B96    16 W. Jackson    1853-54
B97    711-13 and 715 Cameo    1851
*B98    19 E. Duval    1818-19*
*B99    23-25 E. Duval    1815-17*
B100   8 E. Jackson    1846 and 1903
B101   18-22 E. Jackson    1842
B102   714 N. 2nd    1859
B103   749 N. 2nd    1816
B104   725 N. 2nd    1827-28
B105   722 N. 3rd    1814
B106   716-18 N. 3rd    1860
B107   706-8 N. 3rd    1848
*B108   612 N. 3rd    1800 or 1801*
B109   615 N. 2nd    1845
B110   611 N. 2nd    1845
B111   605 and 607 N. 2nd    1848
B112   535½ N. 2nd    1854
B113   211-13 E. Leigh    1842
B114   215 E. Leigh    1833
B115   525 N. 2nd    1848
B116   514 N. 3rd    1829
*B117   204 E. Clay    1848*
B118   211 E. Clay    1859
B119   213 E. Clay    c. 1880
B120   215 E. Clay    1854
B121   217-19 E. Clay    1861
B122   208-12 E. Broad    1860
B123   503-5 N. 3rd    1859
B124   304 E. Clay    1862
B125   306 E. Clay    1861
B126   308 E. Clay    1855
B127   319 E. Clay    c. 1875
B128   522 and 524 N. 4th    1842
B129   308 E. Leigh    1853
B130   300 E. Leigh    1853
B131   609 N. 3rd    1858
B132   613-15 N. 3rd    late 19th cen.
B133   617 N. 3rd    1859
B134   631-33 N. 3rd    1858
B135   701-3 N. 3rd    1858

B136   307 E. Duval   1857 and 1909
B137   726 N. 4th   c. 1860
B138   708 to 722 N. 4th   1852-59
B139   729 N. 4th   1858
B140   709-9½ N. 4th   1858
B141   710 N. 5th   1855
B142   747½-49½ N. 5th (rear)   c. 1858
B143   715 N. 5th   1853
B144   621 N. 4th   c. 1856
B145   405-7 E. Jackson   1856
B146   529 N. 4th   1842
B147   531 N. 4th   1855
B148   408 E. Leigh   1852
*B149   410 E. Leigh   c. 1865*
*B150   608-10 N. 5th   probably 1833*
B151   618-20 N. 5th   c. 1843
B152   627 N. 5th   1848 (demolished 1966)
B153   621 N. 5th   1843
B154   Church, 500 E. Leigh   c. 1900
*B155   Hawes house, 506 E. Leigh   1816 (demolished)*
B156   516 N. 6th   1840-41
B157   509 E. Leigh   c. 1860
B158   507 E. Leigh (rear)   1850
B159   519 N. 5th   1855
B160   524 N. 5th   1846
B161   522 N. 5th   1845
B162   508-18 N. 5th   1860
B163   507 N. 5th   1849
B164   508 E. Clay   1854
B165   407 E. Clay   1851
B166   404 to 412 E. Clay   c. 1870-1880
B167   504 E. Marshall   c. 1858
*B168   The Blues Armory, NE corner Marshall and 6th*
       *1909*
B169   415-17 N. 6th   1857
B170   427 N. 6th   1840
B171   504 N. 6th   1853
B172   Tinsley house, 509 N. 6th   before 1810
B173   515 N. 6th   1853
B174   518 N. 7th   1856
B175   516 N. 7th   1839

B176   512 N. 7th   1839
B177   619-21 N. 6th   1818 (demolished 1965)
B178   625 N. 6th   1848-49
B179   627 N. 6th   1851
B180   632 N. 7th   1838 (demolished 1967)
B181   630 N. 7th   1849
B182   628 N. 7th   c. 1865
B183   624 N. 7th   1861
B184   620 N. 7th   1860
B185   605 to 609 N. 7th   c. 1870
B186   *Richmond Howitzers Armory, 600 block N. 8th*
       *1895*
B187   634-36 N. 8th   1854
B188   *John Marshall house, 402 N. 9th   1788-1791*
B189   *Benj. Watkins Leigh house, 1000 E. Clay*
       *1812-16*
B190   *Wm. H. Grant house, 1008 E. Clay   1857*
B191   *1001 E. Clay   1879*
B192   *Bransford house, 1007 E. Clay   1840*
B193   *Valentine Museum, 1009 E. Clay   c. 1870*
B194   *Wickham house, 1015 E. Clay   1812*
B195   *Samuel Putney house, 1010 E. Marshall   1861*
B196   *Stephen Putney house, 1012 E. Marshall   1859*
B197   *1101 E. Clay   1848*
B198   *Maupin-Maury house, 1105 E. Clay   1846*
B199   *White House of the Confederacy, 1201 E. Clay*
       *1816-18*
B200   *Egyptian Building, E. Marshall and College*
       *1845*
B201   *First African Baptist Church, College at E. Broad*
       *1876*
B202   *Beers house, 1228 E. Broad   1839*
B203   *Monumental Church, 1200 block E. Broad*
       *1812-14*
B204   *First Baptist Church, NW corner E. Broad and*
       *12th   1841*
B205   *Broad Street Methodist Church, NE corner E.*
       *Broad and 10th   1858-59*
B206   12 W. Baker   1813
B207   915-17 St. John   1855
B208   916 St. James   1817

B209    *909 St. James   1845*
B210    1001-3 St. James    1840
B211    1000-1002 N. 1st    1848
B212    1006 N. 1st   1860
B213    1008-10 N. 1st    1848
B214    4 E. Hill    1838
*B215    1115 N. 1st    probably 1816*
B216    908-10 N. 2nd    1859
B217    1011 N. 2nd    1834
B218    1000 N. 3rd    1856
*B219    1013 N. 3rd    1790*
B220    301 E. Preston    1852
B221    306 E. Preston    1858
B222    311-11½ E. Preston    1857
B223    1001-3 N. 4th    1858-59
B224    1009-11 N. 4th    1850
B225    910 N. 5th    1842
B226    913 N. 5th    1857
*B227    Richmond Nursing Home, Hospital St. opposite
        Shockoe Cemetery   1860 and later*
B228    900 N. 3rd    c. 1840
B229    700-708 W. Marshall    1847
B230    710 and 712 W. Marshall    1846
B231    720 W. Marshall    1855
B232    721 W. Clay    1844
B233    713 W. Clay    1859
B234    700 W. Clay    1844-45
B235    706-8 W. Clay    1843
B236    710 W. Clay    1845
B237    718 W. Clay    1845
B238    720 W. Clay    1843
B239    722 W. Clay    1856
B240    724 W. Clay    1844
B241    809 W. Clay    1858-59
B242    813 W. Clay    c. 1870
*B243    815 W. Clay    1859*
B244    808 W. Clay    1842
B245    729-31 Catherine    1860
B246    725 Catherine    1856
B247    713 Catherine    1859
B248    709 Catherine    1853

B249    707 Catherine    c. 1850
B250    705 Catherine    c. 1850
B251    700-702 Catherine    1843
B252    706 Catherine    1843
B253    701 W. Leigh    1844
B254    1504 Brook Ave.    1842
B255    1112 N. 1st    1856
C1    419 W. Broad    1852
C2    316 W. Grace    1859
C3    416 W. Franklin    c. 1900
C4    415 W. Franklin
C5    *400 W. Franklin    c. 1870*
C6    *Commonwealth Club, 401 W. Franklin    1890*
C7    400-406 W. Main    late 19th cen.
C8    *Baltimore Row, 305-9 W. Franklin    c. 1875*
C9    *Lyons house, 301 W. Franklin    1858*
C10    209 W. Canal (rear)    1861
C11    *Daniel Call house, 217 W. Grace    before 1796*
C12    *1019-21 E. Cary    mid-19th cen.*
C13    *211 W. Franklin    1852*
C14    212 W. Franklin    1805-10
C15    206 W. Franklin    late 19th cen.
C16    *Cole Diggs house, 204 W. Franklin    c. 1809*
C17    *200 W. Franklin    c. 1875*
C18    201 W. Franklin    c. 1900
C19    118 W. Grace    1848
C20    113 N. Foushee    1840
C21    *Wm. F. Taylor house, 110 W. Franklin    1845,
altered    1884*
C22    100 W. Franklin    1876
C23    *111 N. Adams*
C24    Church, SE corner E. Franklin and Adams
c. 1904    now University College
C25    Archer Anderson house, 103 W. Franklin    1815
and later
C26    *Jefferson Hotel, 100 block W. Franklin    1895*
C27    13-17 E. Grace    1858
C28    11 S. Adams    (demolished 1966)
C29    *Kent-Valentine house, 12 E. Franklin    1845*
C30    *Linden Row, 100-114 E. Franklin    1847 and
1853*

*C31*    *Bolling Haxall house, 211 E. Franklin    1858*
C32    5 N. 2nd    1846
*C33*    *8-12 N. 2nd    1848*
*C34*    *Crozet house, 100 E. Main    1814-15*
*C35*    *15 E. Franklin    1837*
*C36*    *13 E. Franklin    1847*
*C37*    *11 E. Franklin    1840, altered 1896*
C38    1 E. Franklin    1840 (demolished 1966)
C39    12 E. Main    1837-38 and later
*C40*    *Allen double house, 4-6 E. Main    1836*
*C41*    *1 E. Main    1839 (demolished 1968)*
*C42*    *Ellen Glasgow house, 1 W. Main    1841*
*C43*    *Centenary Methodist Church, 500 block E. Grace    1845, altered 1874*
C44    16 and 18 S. 1st    late 19th cen.
C45    14 S. 1st    1845
C46    106 E. Cary    c. 1900
*C47*    *108 E. Cary    c. 1875*
*C48*    *110 E. Cary    1859*
*C49*    *112 E. Cary    1853*
C50    117 E. Cary    1842
C51    107 E. Cary    1853
C52    105 E. Cary    1854
C53    103 E. Cary    c. 1880
C54    row, 100 block S. 1st    c. 1875
C55    116 S. 1st    1857
C56    14-16 E. Canal    1812-13
C57    124 E. Byrd
C58    8 Maiden Lane    1848
C59    10 Maiden Lane    1848
C60    20 Maiden Lane    1845
C61    22 to 32 Maiden Lane    1838
C62    527 S. Belvidere    1850
C63    529 and 531 S. Belvidere    1857
C64    608 to 614 Church    1849-53
C65    602 Church    1849
C66    522, 524, and 600 Church    1859-62
C67    518-20 Church    c. 1848
C68    516 Church    1853
C69    519 Church    1849
C70    525-29 Church    c. 1870

C71   603 Church   1848
C72   610 S. 1st   1860
C73   602 S. 1st   1848
*C74   322 S. 3rd   1861*
*C75   Pulliam house, 217 S. 3rd   1856*
C76   216 S. 3rd   1848
C77   213-21 S. 4th   c. 1865
C78   209 S. 4th   1854
C79   117 S. 3rd   c. 1885 (demolished 1966)
C80   113-15 S. 3rd   1859
*C81   Henry Coalter Cabell house, 116 S. Third   1847*
C82   106 S. 3rd   1860 (demolished 1965)
C83   12 N. 4th   1842
C84   403 E. Franklin   1859
*C85   Hancock-Caskie house, 2 N. 5th   1808-9*
*C86   Second Presbyterian Church, N. 5th   1847*
*C87   Scott-Clarke house, 9 S. 5th   1841*
*C88   Barret house, 13 S. 5th   1844*
*C89   Norman Stewart house, 707 E. Franklin   1844*
C90   715 and 717 E. Grace   c. 1865
*C91   St. Peter's Church, E. Grace at 8th   1834*
C92   815 E. Broad   1853
*C93   St. Paul's Church, E. Grace at 9th   1844-45*
*C94   Bell Tower, Capitol Square   1824*
*C95   Capitol, Capitol Square   1787, additions 1903-6*
*C96   Washington Monument, Capitol Square   1850-69*
*C97   Governor's Mansion, Capitol Square   1811-12*
*C98   City Hall, Capitol Street between 10th and 11th*
      *1887-94*
*C99   Morson Row, 219-23 Governor   1853*
C100   721-37 E. Main   c. 1900
*C101   First National Bank, SW corner E. Main and 9th*
       *1912*
*C102   911-13 E. Main   c. 1870*
C103   919 and 921 E. Main   late 19th cen.
*C104   Department of Finance, Capitol Square   1895*
C105   910 and 912 E. Main   c. 1870
C106   914 E. Main   c. 1870
C107   916 and 918-20 E. Main   c. 1880
C108   922 and 924 E. Main   late 19th cen.

*C109*   *Custom house, 1000 block E. Main    1858 and later*

C110    1005 E. Main   c. 1910

*C111    1007-13 E. Main    c. 1866*

*C112    1015 E. Main    c. 1870*

C113    1017-19 E. Main   c. 1870

C114    1101-3 E. Main   c. 1870

*C115    1109 E. Main    c. 1870*

*C116·    1111 E. Main    c. 1870*

*C117    1113 E. Main    c. 1870*

C118    1115-17 E. Main   c. 1880

C119    1112 to 1116 E. Main   c. 1870

*C120    1200 E. Main    1893*

C121    1201-5 E. Main   c. 1870

*C122    1207-11 E. Main    1866*

C123    1200 to 1214 E. Cary   c. 1870

*C124    1211 to 1219 E. Cary    c. 1870*

*C125    Watering trough, Shockoe Slip    1909*

*C126    Columbian Block, 1301-7 E. Cary    1871*

*C127    1309-21 E. Cary    c. 1870-80*

C128    1308 and 1310 E. Cary   c. 1870-80

C129    1309 and 1311 E. Main   c. 1870

C130    1313 to 1317 E. Main   c. 1870-80

*C131    1319 to 1323 E. Main    c. 1870-80*

*C132    1300 to 1304 E. Main    c. 1870*

*C133    1306 to 1310 E. Main    c. 1870*

C134    1314 E. Main   c. 1875

C135    1316 to 1320 E. Main   c. 1885

C136    1411 to 1415 E. Main   c. 1870

C137    1417 to 1421 E. Main   late 19th cen.

C138    1423 to 1427 E. Main   late 19th cen. (1423 demolished 1966)

*C139    1441-43 E. Main    1813-14*

*C140    Wortham and McGruder Warehouse, NE corner E. Cary and 15th    1830*

C141    1506 E. Cary   1858

*C142    Whitlock Store, 1523 E. Cary    1812*

C143    Warehouse, 1100 block E. Cary   mid-19th cen. (demolished 1967)

*D1    Main Street Station, 1600 block E. Main    1900*

D2    3 N. 17th   1833

D3      23-27 N. 17th    c. 1853
*D4*     *Scott's Drug Store, 1617 E. Franklin    1852*
D5      1610-12 E. Franklin    1849
D6      Maule-Crew Soap Factory, 113-17 N. 17th    1853
D7      119-21 and 123 N. 17th    1859
D8      127 to 133 N. 17th    1854
D9      1708-10 E. Franklin    1842-44
D10     1719-21 E. Franklin    1817
D11     1731 E. Main    1845
D12     1809 E. Main    1860
D13     12 N. 19th    1844
*D14*    *Masons' Hall, 1805 E. Franklin    1787*
*D15*    *The Old Stone House, 1916 E. Main*
        *before 1783*
*D16*    *John Enders Tobacco Factory, 20-26 N. 20th*
        *1849*
*D17*    *Wm. H. Grant Tobacco Factory, 1900 E. Franklin*
        *1853*
D18     124 N. 20th    c. 1865
D19     113 N. 19th    1817
D20     111 N. 19th    1846
D21     108 N. 19th    1829
*D22*    *1813-15 E. Grace    1818*
D23     1809½-11 E. Grace    1845
*D24*    *Craig house, 1812 E. Grace    between 1784 and*
        *1787*
D25     Chas. Talbot house, 201 N. 19th    1850 (demo-
        lished 1967)
*D26*    *Pace-King house, 205 N. 19th    1860*
D27     213 N. 19th    1852
D28     219 N. 19th    1851 and later
D29     202 to 206 N. 19th    c. 1870-80
D30     208 N. 19th    1846
D31     211, 213, and 215-17 N. 18th    1845 and 1850
D32     216 N. 18th    mid-19th c.
D33     1806-8 and 1810-12 E. Broad    c. 1845
D34     Elm Tree Row, 301 to 311 N. 19th    1854
D35     313-15 N. 19th    1840
*D36*    *Trinity Methodist Church, E. Broad at 20th*
        *1861*
D37     221-23 N. 20th    1855

D38     232 N. 20th    1858

D39     Old Hebrew Cemetery, E. Franklin west of 20th
        1791

D40     2103-5 E. Franklin    1853-54

D41     McGinness house, 2109 E. Franklin    1840

D42     9 N. 21st    1843

D43     2114 E. Main    1853

*D44     Henrico County Court House, E. Main at 22nd
        1896*

D45     2215-19 E. Main    c. 1875

D46     2300 E. Main    1840

D47     2304-8 E. Main    c. 1875

D48     2312 E. Main    1857

D49     2309-11 E. Franklin    1827

D50     2313 E. Franklin    1851

D51     2412-14 E. Main    1869

D52     8 N. 25th    c. 1850

*D53     Yarbrough Factory, 2419 E. Franklin    1853*

D54     2101 E. Broad    1856

D55     2109 E. Broad    1861

D56     2113 E. Broad    1861-62

D57     2115 E. Broad    1855

D58     2201 to 2205 E. Broad    c. 1865-70

*D59     Turpin house, 2209 E. Broad    1861*

*D60     Yarbrough house, 2215 E. Broad    1861*

D61     2200 E. Broad    1822

*D62     2204-6 E. Broad    1845*

*D63     2208-10 E. Broad    1847*

*D64     2214-16 E. Broad    1849-50*

*D65     2300 E. Broad    1850*

D66     2304 E. Broad    1845

D67     2308 E. Broad    1818-24

*D68     2305 E. Broad    1854*

*D69     Carrington Row, 2307-11 E. Broad    1818*

*D70     Whitlock house, 316 N. 24th    1840*

D71     Monte Maria Convent, E. Grace at 22nd    before
        1810

*D72     Hardgrove house, 2300 E. Grace    1849*

*D73     Hilary Baker house, 2302 E. Grace    1810-16*

*D74     Ann Carrington house, 2306 E. Grace    between
        1810 and 1816*

D75    *Harwood and Estes houses, 2308 and 2310 E. Grace    1869*

D76    *2312-14 E. Grace    1885*

D77    *Pollard house, 2316 E. Grace    1885*

D78    2401 E. Grace    c. 1870

D79    *2403 E. Grace    1844*
       *Elmira Shelton house, 2407 E. Grace    1844*

D80    *St. John's Church, E. Broad between 24th and 25th    1741 and later*

D81    *St. Patrick's Church, 215 N. 25th    1859*

D82    213 N. 25th    c. 1870

D83    *John Morris Cottage, 207 N. 25th    1835*

D84    *John Morris Cottage, 2500 E. Grace    c. 1830*

D85    2506-8 E. Grace    1840

D86    2510-12 E. Grace    1840

D87    2514-18 E. Grace    1858

D88    *2519 E. Grace    1862*

D89    *2517 E. Grace    1857*

D90    2515 E. Grace (rear part)    1857

D91    *2513 E. Grace    c. 1865*

D92    *Adams Double House, 2501-3 E. Grace    1809-10*

D93    113-15 N. 25th    1846

D94    318 N. 25th    1849

D95    *316 N. 27th    before 1814*

D96    2618 E. Broad    1855

D97    2718 E. Broad    c. 1862

D98    2711 E. Broad    1846

D99    2717 E. Broad    1858

D100   307 N. 28th    1862

D101   314 N. 29th    1860

D102   312 N. 29th    1860

D103   219 N. 28th    1851

D104   *215 and 217 N. 28th    1852 and 1858*

D105   2607 E. Grace    1840

D106   *Andrew Ellett house, 2702 E. Grace    1829*

D107   2706 E. Grace    1860

D108   2703 E. Grace    1844

D109   2705 E. Grace    1804

D110   2715 E. Grace    c. 1870

D111   *White-Taylor house, 2717 E. Grace    1839, altered    c. 1881*

D112　*Bodeker house, 2801 E. Grace　1852*
D113　*2800-2802 E. Grace　1862*
D114　2815 E. Grace　1852
D115　2820 and 2822 E. Grace　1858-59
D116　113 N. 29th　1863
D117　2921 Williamsburg Ave.　mid-19th cen.
D118　105 Ash　1819
D119　*3017 Williamsburg Ave.　1799-1802*
D120　*3017-19 Libby Terrace　1857*
D121　2916 Libby Terrace　c. 1865
D122　2910 Libby Terrace　1861
D123　*Luther Libby house, 1 N. 29th　1850*
D124　*Wm. Hancock house, 11½ N. 29th　1868*
D125　*19 N. 29th　1850*
D126　*107 N. 29th　1857*
D127　109 N. 29th　1860
D128　2818-20 E. Franklin　c. 1885
D129　*Confederate Soldiers and Sailors Monument, Libby Hill Park　1894*
D130　*2718 E. Franklin　1839*
D131　2714 E. Franklin　1865
D132　2701-5 E. Franklin　c. 1900
D133　2614-18 E. Franklin　c. 1875
D134　*2617 E. Franklin　1856*
D135　*2611 E. Franklin　1857*
D136　*2603-5 E. Franklin　1858*
D137　*2601 E. Franklin　1857*
D138　*2602 E. Franklin　1856*
D139　*2600 E. Franklin　1855-56*
D140　*Anthony Turner house, 2520 E. Franklin between 1803 and 1810*
D141　2521 E. Franklin　1858
D142　509-13 Mosby　mid-19th cen.
D143　529 Mosby　1850
D144　531-33 Mosby 1848
D145　600 N. 21st　1853
D146　604 N. 21st　1849
D147　616 N. 21st　1841
D148　609-11 N. 21st　1859
D149　607 N. 21st　1855
D150　605 N. 21st　1853

D151   601 N. 21st   1854
D152   529 N. 21st   1859
D153   521-23 and 525-27 N. 21st   1859
D154   2108 and 2110 E. Leigh   1857 and 1859
D155   604 N. 22nd   1848
D156   2115 M   1847
D157   2113 M   1856
D158   605-7 N. 22nd   c. 1860
D159   609 N. 22nd   1853
D160   611 N. 22nd   1859
D161   2118 and 2120 M   1856
D162   2116 M   1860
D163   2114 M   1859
D164   2121 Pleasants   1857-59
D165   2117-19 Pleasants   c. 1860
D166   2107 and 2109 Pleasants   1861
D167   2103-5 Pleasants   c. 1885
D168   2108 to 2114 Pleasants   c. 1875
D169   709-11 N. 21st   1847
D170   713 N. 21st   1846-56
D171   SW corner Venable and 21st   c. 1870
D172   Church, SE corner Venable and 21st
D173   2113 Venable   1854
D174   2117-19 Venable   c. 1860
*D175   2121 Venable   1854*
D176   Apostolic Church, NW corner Venable and 22nd
       c. 1900
D177   2200 and 2202-4 Pleasants   c. 1865
D178   SE corner, Venable and Jessamine   c. 1847
D179   2223 and 2225 Venable   1839
D180   2239-41 Venable   1850
D181   2302 Venable   1855
D182   2400 Venable   1856
D183   2410 Venable   c. 1825
D184   2427 Venable   1840
D185   2505 Q   1847
D186   2507-9 Q   1856
D187   1005 N. 25th   1851
D188   911 N. 24th   1860
D189   909 N. 24th   c. 1841
D190   910 N. 25th   1855-56

D191   902 N. 25th   1859
D192   820 N. 25th   1859-60
D193   817-9 N. 25th   1860
D194   Union Hill Chapel, 812 N. 25th   1843
D195   802 N. 25th   1856
D196   800 N. 25th   1856
D197   728 N. 25th   1854
D198   709-11 N. 24th   1848
D199   713-25 N. 24th   1860
D200   717-19 N. 24th   1854
D201   723 N. 24th   1859
D202   725 N. 24th   1854
D203   727 N. 24th   1855
D204   Cedar Street Memorial Baptist Church, 24th and
       N   c. 1890
D205   801 and 803 N. 24th   c. 1855
D206   805 N. 24th   1856
D207   817-19 N. 24th   1860
D208   814-16 and 818-20 N. 24th   c. 1855
D209   812 N. 24th   c. 1855
D210   2316 N   1854
D211   2312 N. 1846
D212   805-5½ N. 23rd   1846
D213   811 N. 23rd   1847
D214   813 N. 23rd   1851
*D215   821 N. 23rd   1849*
D216   814 N. 23rd   c. 1853
D217   815 Jessamine   c. 1850
D218   813 Jessamine   1850
D219   807-9 Jessamine   1846-47
D220   2228 and 2230 N   c. 1850
D221   721 N. 23rd   1847
D222   705 N. 23rd   1846
D223   701 N. 23rd   1848
D224   622 N. 23rd   1854 and later
D225   619 N. 23rd   1854
D226   613 N. 23rd   1851
D227   611 N. 23rd   1850
D228   609 N. 23rd   1854
D229   607 N. 23rd   1851
D230   2315 M   1856

D231   2317 and 2319 M   1853 and 1856
D232   2411 M   mid-19th cen.
D233   519 N. 24th   1854-56
D234   511 N. 24th   1856
D235   508-10 N. 24th   1861
D236   500 N. 24th   1855
D237   2220 E. Marshall   1860
D238   2324 E. Marshall   1853
D239   NW corner E. Marshall and 25th   early 20th cen.
D240   2506-8 E. Marshall   1859
*D241   2606 E. Marshall   1814*
D242   2515 E. Clay   1851
D243   500 N. 26th   1859
D244   502 and 504 N. 26th   1845
D245   507½ N. 25th   1855
*D246   Leigh Street Baptist Church, SE corner E. Leigh and 25th 1853*
D247   510 N. 25th   1853
D248   Masonic Lodge, SW corner E. Leigh and 25th c. 1900
D249   2502-4 E. Leigh   1849
D250   607-9 N. 25th   1855
D251   621 N. 25th   1844
*D252   700 N. 26th   c. 1852*
D253   700 N. 27th   c. 1865
D254   701 N. 27th   1855
D255   700 N. 28th   1856
*D256   618 and 620 N. 27th   1843 and 1847*
D257   625 N. 26th   1856
D258   617-19 N. 26th   1841
D259   600-602 N. 27th   1860
D260   2605-7 E. Leigh   1847
*D261   509 N. 27th   1817-18*
*D262   501 N. 27th   before 1819*
D263   2706 E. Clay   1844
D264   419 N. 27th   1855
D265   411 N. 27th   1858
*D266   407 N. 27th   before 1812*
*D267   405 N. 27th   1835*
*D268   Wills's Store, 401 N. 27th   1813-15*
D269   413 N. 28th   1860

D270    2813-15 M    1846
D271    615 N. 29th    1834
D272    623 N. 30th    1843
D273    601 N. 30th    1857
*D274    510 N. 29th    between 1816 and 1820*
D275    500 N. 29th    1860
D276    2901 E. Clay    1860
D277    2905 and 2907 E. Clay    1860 and 1861
D278    2919 E. Clay    1862
D279    425 N. 32nd    probably 1854
D280    2721 E. Broad    1857
D281    3116 M    1858
D282    3213-15 N    1843
D283    Pleasant Oaks, 3700 P    before 1819

# Index

Proper names appearing in parentheses following street addresses are supplied from Mary Wingfield Scott's *Houses of Old Richmond* (1941) and *Old Richmond Neighborhoods* (1950).